Hope and Healing
for Transcending Loss

Hope and Healing
for Transcending Loss

Meditations for Those Who Are Grieving

Ashley Davis Bush, LICSW

Photographs by Richard Evans

Conari Press

Cover Photo: Slivsarenko Luliia/Shutterstock
Layout & Design: Maureen Forys, Happenstance Type-O-Rama

Mango is an active supporter of authors' rights to free speech and artistic
expression in their books. The purpose of copyright is to encourage authors to
produce exceptional works that enrich our culture and our open society.

For permission requests, please contact the publisher at:
Mango Publishing Group
2850 S Douglas Road, 2nd Floor
Coral Gables, FL 33134 USA
info@mango.bz

For special orders, quantity sales, course adoptions and corporate sales, please
email the publisher at sales@mango.bz. For trade and wholesale sales, please
contact Ingram Publisher Services at customer.service@ingramcontent.com or
+1.800.509.4887.

Hope & Healing for Transcending Loss: Daily Meditations for Those Who
Are Grieving

Library of Congress Cataloging-in-Publication Data available upon request.
ISBN: (print) 978-1-57324-667-5
BISAC: SEL010000, SELF-HELP / Death, Grief, Bereavement

Printed in the United States of America

To all those in emotional pain,
may this book be a light in the darkness

*Death doesn't end the relationship; it simply forges a
new type of relationship—one based not on physical
presence but on memory, spirit, and love . . .*

—Ashley Davis Bush, *Transcending Loss*

Contents

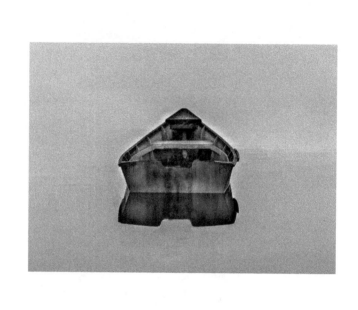

Light in the Darkness

I was twenty-five when I sat in my first session—my first session, that is, in which I was the therapist. With only a month of social work schooling under my belt, I was assigned to my first client, Joan.

It might have been a bewildering encounter given my inexperience, but instead it was transformative. Joan was a middle-aged woman assigned to me for grief counseling. Her beloved sister had been murdered by a handyman in their own home.

I sat with Joan through her tears and I listened. I asked questions. I listened some more. I allowed myself to be touched by her sorrow, and I provided a container for her pain. When I presented this case to my fledgling colleagues, they said, "Oh, how can you work with her? Her story is so depressing."

And yet, curiously, I felt at ease with Joan and her deep sorrow. During our first session together, there was a 'click' of recognition that I was being called to work with the bereaved. And so, for the last twenty-five years, I have done just that.

I have sat with countless widows and widowers, from young to old. I have offered tissues to bereaved parents in their inconsolable grief. I have normalized, educated, listened to, and championed grievers who felt tremendous pain and still chose life.

In fact, I became so immersed in this calling that I studied the grieving process and wrote a book about it—*Transcending Loss*. In the decades since its publication, the grieving process has not changed: Grief is painful and needs to be felt just as love is eternal and needs to be celebrated.

However, with the rise of the Internet, a new dawn has arrived in which grievers have many more options for sharing their grief and connecting to others. This has been an exciting development, because grievers can now bond with other grievers around the world in therapeutic ways.

In 2009, I began the Facebook forum "Transcending Loss" as a way to reach out to those who grieve. The forum featured short, daily reflections as a starting point for grievers from around the world to share their stories and comfort each other. In just a few years, the forum grew from several hundred participants to over twenty-five thousand. This book rose out of that experience. I became keenly aware that short, daily words of hope and comfort make a real difference to people on the grief journey.

As I continue to interact with grievers from around the world, I am again reminded of the universality of grief. And although each journey is unique, there are many common experiences.

As you read through the year, you will encounter recurring themes that reflect the seven essential lessons of loss:

1. *Grief is a normal reaction.* Grief is the natural emotional and physical response to the death of a loved one. Although our society desperately wants to avoid the messiness of deep sorrow, there is no way out except through the pain. Typical numbing techniques such as medications, alcohol, and food are only temporary distractions to dull the pain.

   Letting ourselves grieve by going directly into the pain—in manageable doses over a long period of time—is healing. Avoiding the pain simply forces it to go deep into the heart, where it subtly affects emotional and physical health.

2. *Grief is hard work*. Grief isn't easy and it isn't pretty. It involves tears, sleepless nights, pain, sorrow, and a heartache that knocks you to your knees. It can be hard to concentrate, hard to think clearly, hard to read, and easy to forget all the details of life that everyone else seems to remember. Grievers frequently feel that they're going crazy, and they sometimes wish to die. This doesn't mean that they're actively suicidal; it just means that they're grieving.

3. *Grief doesn't offer closure*. Closure is an idea that we like because we want to tie up our emotional messes with a bow and put them in the back of a closet. But grief refuses to play this game. Grief tends toward healing, not closure. In other words, the funeral can be healing. Visiting a gravesite can be healing. Performing rituals, writing in journals, making pilgrimages to special sites—all of these things can be personally meaningful and healing, but they will not bring closure. Closure is relevant to business deals but not to the human heart.

4. *Grief is lifelong*. Although we all want quick fixes and short-term solutions, grief won't accommodate us. Many people want grief to be over in a few weeks or a few months, and certainly within a year. And yet, many grievers know that the second year is actually

harder than the first. Why? Because the shock has worn off and the reality of the pain has truly sunk in.

I let grievers know that the impact of grief is lifelong just as the influence of love is also lifelong. No matter how many years go by, there will be occasional days when grief bursts through with a certain rawness. There will be days, even a decade later, when sadness crosses over you like a storm cloud. And likely, every day going forward will involve some memory, some connection to missing your beloved.

5. *You as a griever need to stay connected to the deceased.* While some might find it odd or uncomfortable to keep talking about the deceased loved one, or find it disconcerting to see photographs of those who have passed on, it is healthy to keep the connection alive. My heart goes out to a generation or more of grievers who were told to cut ties with their deceased loved ones, to banish all remnants of them, to pretend as if they never existed. Such unwitting cruelty! Honor their birthdays and departure days. Know that their physical presence may be gone from this earth, but that they remain in relationship to you in a new way, beyond form, a way based on spirit and love.

6. *You as a griever are changed forever.* If you expect to eventually be back to your old self, you will be quite

disappointed. Grief, like all major life experiences, changes a person irrevocably. Think about it for a moment. Would you expect to remain unchanged after getting an education, getting married, having a baby, getting divorced, or changing careers? Life is full of experiences that add to the compost mixture of your life, creating rich and fertile soil. Similarly, grief teaches you about life, about death, about pain, about love, and about impermanence. While some people are changed in a way that makes them bitter and shut down, it is possible to use grief as a springboard for compassion, wisdom, and openheartedness.

7. *You as a griever can choose transcendence.* Seeing one's grief from a larger perspective, holding pain in a larger context, allows it to be bearable and gives it meaning. Perhaps it means reaching out to others who suffer. Perhaps it means giving to a cause that will result in helping others. Grievers who choose transcendence recognize that they are not alone, that they share in the human condition, and that they are amongst all people who experience love and loss. They use their pain in a way that touches others. The pain is still there, of course, but it is transformed.

I invite you to use this book, reading it every day, as a companion, as a guide, as a hand holding yours along this path called grief. May it soothe and calm you, reminding you that you are not alone. May it provide you with hope and healing.

Hope and Healing

for Transcending Loss

January 1

We often think of grief closing us down as we draw inward to heal, as we withdraw from life. But to what is grief opening you up? Are you more open to dying, more open to spiritual phenomenon? Have you opened yourself to other grievers, to experiencing love in a deeper way? Are you more open to the mysteries of the universe? Look and discover how you are becoming more open to life. If you haven't experienced this yet, this year will offer opportunities to "open." Trust the process.

Today

Close your eyes and repeat the words, "I am open to new experiences and new feelings this year."

January 2

Recovering from grief is not a matter of "letting go" of your loved one—quite the contrary. Living with loss means that you hold on in a new way. You live every day with your loved one in your heart, woven into your soul, surrounding you with presence. And then you still choose to move forward living the life that is left to you.

Today

Know that you hold on with love.

January 3

People will admire your strength, but usually what they mean is your ability to appear "together," to be stoic, to wear a mask that indicates, "I'm okay." What people don't realize is that real strength comes in facing the grief, falling apart, crying, and letting yourself *feel*. You are strong every day you choose to be alive. But let your real strength be in facing the feelings so that you can move through the process.

Today

Say, "I am strong" as you allow yourself to grieve.

January 4

Some people are tempted to shut down their grief, put it in a box, and stuff it in the back of the closet. There is a price to pay for avoiding grief: You might get sick, both emotionally and physically. Instead, seek the balance of first letting grief in and then taking a rest from the feelings. Take grief in small doses so that the feelings are being absorbed rather than avoided. Your health depends on it.

Today

Choose to experience your grief, even in small doses.

January 5

Memories can feel double-edged. They can be painful, sharp, highlighting your loss . . . or they can remind you of wonderful times, deep love, and life lived. Be open to your many memories, a flower field of times that connect you to your loved one. Hold each memory with reverence, and let yourself savor the love.

Today

Recall a favorite moment with your loved one.

January 6

When you lose someone you love dearly, your heart simply cracks and breaks. You will likely feel truly heartbroken, almost as if there is a deep ache in your body. Some days all you will feel is this sorrow, this agony. Let yourself feel the heartbreak. You must feel in order to heal.

Today

How would you describe the condition of your heart?

January 7

What the caterpillar sees as death we know is a transition to the beautiful butterfly. We have that perspective. However, when it comes to our own death—or the death of our dear ones—we don't have such a clear perspective. Remember the butterfly and know that we don't have the whole picture. Breathe. Trust.

Today

Can you open yourself to mystery?

January 8

In the old days of grief counseling, grievers were advised to cut their emotional attachment to the deceased, to forget and move on. Can you imagine? Now we understand that deep love and strong attachments never end. It's never a matter of ending a relationship. Grief is a matter of integrating a different relationship into your life, one of spirit and formlessness. Death cannot break the bonds of deep, true love.

Today

Know that true love always transcends loss.

January 9

You may be a different person because of your loss, but you are also a different person because of your love. Think about how your life expanded by loving your dear one and receiving their love. Think about how empty life would be if you had never known them and experienced the blessing of them. Their love is still with you, woven inextricably into your soul.

Today

Who would you be if you hadn't known your loved one?

January 10

You may frequently wonder, how am I going to survive this? How can I endure this unbearable pain and sorrow? Do not think ahead; simply draw your attention back to one moment at a time, one breath at a time, and let it expand into one day at a time. Keep your focus narrow. Day will add to day, and you will live your way into the future. But for now, only this moment.

Today

Breathe. Focus on the in-breath, focus on the space between breaths, and focus on the out-breath.

January 11

Be gentle with yourself. The work of grief is exhausting. You may find that you are forgetful, that you cannot concentrate, and that you are fatigued easily. Grieving requires so much energy! Cut yourself some slack without judgment. Be extra kind to you.

Today

What kind gesture can you offer yourself today?

January 12

How would your beloved want you to live your remaining days? What would they say to you about your time left on the planet? Even as you grieve, know that life is to be lived. You will find a way to embrace life, even with a hole in your heart, because that is what they would wish for you.

Today

Choose life today in honor of your dear one.

January 13

Tears are a way to move emotion through the body. You never need to apologize for your tears. They are emotion overflowing. Let yourself cry in the shower, in the car, in your bedroom. It's far easier to let the tears flow than to try to hold them back. Release and let emotion flush through you.

Today

Let yourself cry.

January 14

Some days will feel like "bad" days, and some days will feel like "good" days. Try not to judge the days too much. Just know that some days the grief is close to the surface and may overflow with strong emotion. Other days, the love feels stronger than the loss and you're able to smile. All of these days are part of the process.

Today

Just let today be what it needs to be.

January 15

Find people who will not be afraid to share memories of your loved one. Be bold in asking friends, family, and colleagues, "What is your favorite memory of _____?" It is healing to remember, to revisit, and even to share a tear or two. Memories are a treasure trove, like golden nuggets that you will want to hold close to your heart.

Today

Hold a memory close to your heart.

January 16

It often isn't discussed, but it's very common to have signs or communications with those who have left the planet. Anything is possible, from strange electrical occurrences (lights turning on or off), to animal sightings, to dream visitations, to pennies appearing out of nowhere. Accept each signal as a gift, a loving intention. Your loved one wants you to know that they are still with you, now and always.

Today

Be open to receiving a sign from your dear one. If you long for this but it hasn't happened yet, just be open and curious.

January 17

I have heard grievers say that they didn't see color or taste food for *years* after a major loss. But then, at some point, color came back . . . taste was possible. Smiles happened. Laughter, too. Life returned. As you learn to live with loss and integrate sorrow into your heart on a daily basis, be open to the possibility that life is still worth living.

Today

Breathe in these words: "Life has color."

January 18

Love is a gift. Love is such an immense gift, in fact, that it transcends time, place, distance, and space . . . it even transcends death. Know that the love you have given and received is now a part of you. This love permeates your soul and will illumine your experience of the world. Even as grief weighs heavy, know that love can lift you with its lightness.

Today

Give thanks for the gift of love.

January 19

Many grievers are afraid that they're doing it "wrong." Trust in your own process . . . if you need to cry, to write, to sit, to stare, let yourself be with your experience. Everyone has their own way of "doing" grief, so let yourself do what feels right and natural for you. Let grief move around you, over you, and through you.

Today

Let your process be unique to you.

January 20

Do not expect to one day return to your old self. Grief has changed you irrevocably. You are growing into a new self, day by day. This new self may be fearful, bitter, and shut down . . . or this new self may be full of increased compassion, heightened understanding, and deep love. Be open to such a transformation. Be open to letting grief break open your heart so that light comes through the cracks.

Today

Let light shine today through the cracks of your broken heart.

January 21

Grief comes in waves—sometimes giant tsunami waves
that knock you down and leave you flattened. Other
times the waves are gentle lapping rhythms. But the waves
keep coming, and keep receding . . . eventually spacing
themselves out. Once you start to ride the waves, you will
feel less out of control. Expect them and be ready, knowing that the rhythms will come and go.

Today

Ride the waves of grief today without resistance.

January 22

Your loved one is with you . . . when you cry, when you
laugh. Your loved one is with you . . . when you hide from
life, when you embrace life. Your loved one is with you . . .
when you think of them, when you think of something else.
No matter what, your loved one is with you, always.

Today

Know that your dear one is with you, now and forever.

January 23

After a star dies, its light continues to shine for millions of years. So it is with your loved one. Their light just keeps shining, especially through the ones who are still here. Look and you will see that their light still shines all around you . . . and even shines through you.

Today

Watch for ways that the light of your loved one still shines.

January 24

You can't force it to be spring if it is winter. If you are in the winter of your grief, let yourself hibernate. Stop fighting the fact that it's winter. Rest in your grief; let it be. While winter days will still reappear now and then for the rest of your life, spring thaw will start to happen as time goes by. Spring flowers will even bloom again. But for now, be in your winter.

Today

Be where you are.

January 25

Notice the ways in which you are absorbing aspects of your dear one into your personality: Do you tell their jokes? Cook their recipes? Listen to their music? Have their attitude? Support their sports teams? Are you inspired by their courage, their laughter, their example? Let them become a part of you as you carry on their legacy.

Today

Reflect on ways that you are similar to your loved one.

January 26

Do not expect "closure" from your grief, or even a natural "end." You will not get over this the way you would get over an illness. You can expect to feel pain, to integrate loss into your life, and to continually be sideswiped by sorrow. However, the intensity will change over time. You can also expect to experience love as an ever-present infusion into your being. So, while you won't have complete "closure" on your grief, you can know that you'll also not have closure on the love, the impact, and the presence of your dear one.

Today

Let go of the idea of "closure."

January 27

Grief may well be one of the most surprising journeys you've ever been on. You could be surprised at the intensity of your pain. You are likely surprised by some people's reactions to your pain. It's possibly surprising how grief is a lifelong adaptation to your loss. And you may find surprise in the places that grief can take you—places of growth, love, and compassion. Try to be open to the unexpected.

Today

In what ways is grief surprising you?

January 28

If you think that death means your relationship is over, you are wrong. You are still in a relationship with your loved one, and you always will be. You will continue to love, to cherish, to remember, even to talk out loud to them. Your relationship is transformed to one without physical form, but it is nevertheless a relationship. Let it unfold into something new.

Today

Know that your relationship is eternal.

January 29

You are more than your grief, more than your pain, more than your sorrow. You are a being of light who can tap into a great energy that is within you and beyond you. Let this time of year be a time to hold your grief and your light simultaneously. Dwell in stillness and know that the light connects you now and always to all those you have loved and lost.

Today

Connect to the light that is at the core within you.

January 30

Grief asks you to be a turtle. Like a turtle, you need to retreat into your shell to rest. Let yourself do so. Pull into that shell for respite. There will be a time to come out of the shell, for short periods and then longer periods. For now, know that it is okay to draw inward.

Today

Give yourself permission to pull into your shell.

January 31

Just when you feel you cannot bear any more sadness, you will notice some tenderness, some beauty, some light. Look around you and begin to notice the smallest signs that, in the midst of sorrow, bring you a measure of comfort. Perhaps it's a hug, a card, a gesture, a musical note, a photo, a hand holding yours. These are the little lifelines that help you hold on when you wonder whether you can. You can and you will.

Today

Open your eyes and notice simple comforts around you.

February 1

What if your final conversation was not a heartfelt, loving moment? What if your final conversation was an argument or an unkind word? It's time to forgive yourself for being human. You didn't know that it would be your last interaction—nor did they. Your ticket to freedom is forgiving yourself. Yes, you wish it could have unfolded differently, but you are left with the reality of what actually happened. They have forgiven you; now it's your turn.

Today

Breathe in acceptance, breathe out guilt. Breathe in forgiveness, breathe out regret.

February 2

What happens to the pain over time? It changes and evolves and transforms and softens. However, some days, even many years later, you may experience a sharp edge—maybe as sharp as in the first few months or years of your grief. This is normal for those living with loss.

Today

Remember that in spite of the occasional sharp edge, your grief will soften over time.

February 3

Writing about your experience can be incredibly profound. There is something about pulling the feelings through your body with words and then putting them down on paper that is quite therapeutic. Keeping a journal becomes tangible evidence of the journey that you are on. Let your journal be a place of honesty and pure expression.

Today

Write your answer to this prompt: "Today, when I think about my loss, I feel . . ."

February 4

There is no doubt that you would much rather have your dear one's physical presence next to you. That is a given. However, imagine how much worse it would be if their love was gone as well. But no . . . their love for you is imprinted upon you. Their love for you continues to motivate, console, and comfort you. Likewise, your love for them is ever vibrant and intense. True love never dies.

Today

Know that love wraps around you, sits beside you, and shines upon you and out from within you.

February 5

Grieving requires a great deal of patience. There is the necessary patience for coping with the process: the ups and downs, the range of feelings, the ebbing pain. There is the stretch of patience for others who do not understand your experience and perpetually say the wrong thing. And there is the patience required for enduring life while you're waiting to reunite with your loved one in eternity.

Today

Let yourself rest in the moment. Be patient. The next moment is already on its way.

February 6

Immediately after your loved one's death, and even up to a few months later, it's typical to get a *lot* of support and sympathy. Then people return to their lives, and you are left with your heartbreak. Make sure that you continue to find people who will support you as time goes on. Similarly, be the friend who checks in with other grievers six, twelve, and eighteen months later. It's vital to create your own web of support.

Today

Do you know a griever whom you can contact today?

February 7

Sometimes, it's easy to cast blame for your loved one's death. You might blame a perpetrator, a doctor, or a legal system. The impulse is strong to find someone to pay for this loss. However, vengeance will not bring back your beloved. And it might keep you stuck in a sort of bitterness. Many have experienced that even when justice is served, a hollowness settles into their hearts.

Today

Question your desire to blame others as a possible distraction from your own grief. Let yourself sit with the unvarnished reality of loss.

February 8

Grief is not the entire puzzle of your life. Yes, the feelings are huge and overwhelming on many days. However, grief is merely a *piece* in the puzzle of your life. You have love, a spacious soul, and many opportunities for growth. You are still here for a reason . . . you are lifting off every day into a life of which grief is a part (but not the whole).

Today

Know that the puzzle of your life has many important pieces.

February 9

Sometimes, you don't want to remember the irritating aspects of your loved one . . . the annoying traits, the arguments, the immaturities. Guess what? We're all human, and therefore subject to various flaws and imperfections. It's okay to remember what you don't miss as well as what you do. Embracing the foibles of your dear one is just as important as honoring their virtues. Everyone is a package deal.

Today

You have permission to remember all aspects of your dear one.

February 10

Grief is a teacher in your life. It's a teacher that you didn't ask for and don't particularly want. However, it is now a part of your life. Over time, your relationship with grief will change and evolve. Rather than seeing grief as the enemy, see it as an instructor. See what lessons it has for you about living, and honoring life. See what lessons it has for you about dying.

Today

Be curious and ask grief, What are you trying to teach me?

February 11

It's very natural to continue to feel as if you could just pick up the phone and call them . . . or drop by their house and talk to them. You may find yourself expecting to see them in their old chair or even sitting at the table. It takes a long time to register that their physical form is no longer here. And as you are reminded over and over again, it can feel like a fresh shock.

Today

Know that it's not easy to wrap your mind around the truth that their form is gone from this planet.

February 12

Acute grief can last from weeks to months to years. Eventually, it fades to subtle grief. Think of acute grief as a symphony, front stage and captivating. Subtle grief is more like a cocktail pianist playing background music. Grief changes, shifts, and plays a new tune, but it doesn't disappear completely.

Today

Welcome the music of grief in your life.

February 13

Valentine's Eve, holidays, birthdays, and anniversaries
can be tough. Grief, of course, needs no special occasion,
but the anticipation of a holiday is often especially poignant. Allow yourself to breathe through the feelings.
You *will* get through this holiday, this one and future ones.
It's another day to hold love and loss side by side.

Today

Watch, experience, and accept your grief as it unfolds.

February 14

Amidst your sorrow, remember that love is the greatest
energy we know. It helps us expand, open, give, and bless.
Look at how the love you have for your dear one can continue to express itself now—perhaps in new and surprising ways. Love keeps your dear one close. Love can help
you reengage with life.

Today

Let your heart fill with love even in the midst of sorrow.

February 15

There is a time for every season . . . a time to mourn . . . a time to cry. Don't resist nature's call to retreat, to draw inward. It's important to let yourself feel your feelings and be in the grief. There will be a time for another season. Until then, follow nature's example.

Today

Remember that your feelings will cycle around, like the seasons.

February 16

The journey of grief is not a direct, linear route. You take a step forward, another back, and the path turns just when you least expect it. You thought you were going strong in one direction, and then you find that you must stop and rest. Be gentle with yourself. There is no goal or endpoint. Your journey may even take you down an unexpected path.

Today

Consider starting a grief journal. Let your feelings of each day make their mark on paper. Over time, you'll be amazed how love and grief companion together on this long and winding road.

February 17

They say that time heals all wounds, but that isn't completely true: It's how you spend that time that makes the difference. If you spend the time avoiding your grief, it only goes underground, where it makes you sick. If you spend the time getting increasingly bitter, time only makes you miserable. However, if you spend the time facing your grief, and even befriending it, if you spend your time embracing love and creating a new relationship with your dear one, then time will help you heal.

Today

What are you doing with your time?

February 18

Grief will flood you when you least expect it. You might be having a good day and then suddenly find yourself in tears. It could feel like grief blindsides you over and over again. Don't resist these outbursts of feeling—just sit with them and let them pass.

Today

Can you allow the grief to rise to the surface when it needs to?

February 19

You just don't know where grief is going to lead you. At the very least, it will introduce you to new people and to a deeper compassion for emotional pain. Think of those you have met in grief groups or on Internet support communities. True, you would always rather have your loved one back, but be open to where the path of grief will take you and whose path you will cross because of it.

Today

Whom have you met as a direct result of your loss?

February 20

We live in a world that doesn't like pain. We too might be tempted to turn from it, to keep a stiff upper lip. But grief asks us to touch pain, to sit with pain, to ask it to tea. Being with your sorrow is brave and courageous. Not only is there nothing wrong with you for feeling your pain, know that it takes strength to venture into this frightening territory.

Today

Remember that grief is borne of love.

February 21

While it's true that you're irrevocably changed after a major loss, it's also true that you were irrevocably changed for knowing and loving your dear one. Think about how they influenced you, changed you, and impacted you with their personality. Imagine if you had never known them. Both love and grief have shaped you and will continue to do so.

Today

Remember that you are the sum of both having lost and having loved.

February 22

No matter how many years go by—even if you've made meaning of your loss and moved on to a new you, a new life, with your loved one ever in your heart—there will be days when the grief feels as raw as if the loss has just occurred. This is normal. Honor the retriggered grief— ride the wave, and watch it ebb and flow like the tide.

Today

Close your eyes and take a moment to follow your breath as it flows in and out.

February 23

Your loved one was and is an extraordinary gift in your life. Remember, the gift does not become less valuable simply because the form and packaging have changed. Although it may seem as if the gift have been wrenched from you, in fact, the beautiful aspects of the gift continue to shower down upon you.

Today

Give a gift in honor of your loved one.

February 24

Grief has an amazing ability to cut through the superficialities of life. Life takes on stark meaning when you realize how fragile it is. Life, in fact, never quite looks the same once you've encountered the sharp reality of death. The question is, How will this awareness shape your remaining days?

Today

Reflect on what matters to you now.

February 25

You will find that some people simply do not understand your process, your grief. They may say things that appear insensitive or unkind (such as suggesting that you "move on"). Know that it is not their wish to be unsupportive. We live in a pain-averse culture, and people will go to great lengths to minimize and mask it. Rather than feel insulted, use each opportunity as a chance to educate people about love, about grief, and about pain. One day, they too will understand.

Today

Tell someone about how the grief experience is for you.

February 26

Your goal is not to forget about your loved one or move into a life in which they don't exist. Your goal, for now, is to be with grief. Your goal, with time, is to learn to live with loss and integrate it into your life. Your goal, now and always, is to hold your loved one close, letting the love you share radiate within and beyond you.

Today

Hold your hand over your heart. Feel the love.

February 27

Grieving, the work of processing the pain of loss, is a bit like a job. It takes up your time and your energy, especially in the first few years after a major loss. Know that as you cry, as you mourn, as you draw into your shell, you are doing your job very well.

Today

Be assured that when you do the work of grieving, you are courageous.

February 28

What does it mean to "move on"? It means to keep your loved one ever in your heart as you begin to open to life and reconnect to the living. Over time, slowly, when the choice comes to keep living, you will "move forward" *with* your loved one, who is ever a part of you. If you're not there yet, be patient. If you're getting closer, be gentle. If you're already there, keep your heart open.

Today

Know that as you move forward, you carry your beloved with you.

March 1

There is no expiration date on grieving. Even if your loss happened years ago, now could be the time to revisit feelings that you didn't honor way back when. Know that grief can be opened, examined, felt, and processed many years after the loss. It's never too late to grieve. Perhaps now is the time.

Today

Look back in time . . . Is there a loss from the past that is waiting for your attention?

March 2

Notice how you are supported in your grief . . . through friends who understand, family, online communities, religious groups, mentors, and counselors. Know that needing support is not a weakness—it is a sign of being human. We all need and deserve to be supported on our journey.

Today

Call a friend and let them know how you're really feeling.

March 3

It is natural after a loss to ask the question, "Why?" However, we will likely not know the answer to that question in this lifetime. A different question to ask is, "What now?" Living into the answer of that question means to learn, grow, keep your heart open, reach out to others, keep your relationship with your dear one vibrant, find meaning, and turn your attention to those still here.

Today

Ask the question, "What now?" and be open to living into an answer.

March 4

Give yourself time to grieve, to ride the waves of pain,
to share with others, to reach out, and to draw in. Give
yourself time to turn toward grief, to express your feelings, to learn, and then, bit by bit, to begin to embrace
life. Let yourself be in the process of grief and know that
you will be supported by a love that is woven into the fabric of your being.

Today

Give your grief time.

March 5

With grief, it is as if you are living in a well of tears. The
well is deep with the accumulated pain of profound loss.
However, at the bedrock of the well is a foundation of
gratitude. It may be difficult to contact it, but gratitude
is there. Aren't you grateful for having had this beloved
person in your life, for their love, for your love for them,
for having had the privilege of knowing and loving them?

Today

Remember that gratitude is your bedrock.

March 6

The Old English root of the word *bereavement* means "to rob." You will often feel like you have been robbed of your loved one, of precious time with them. Know that it is normal to have this feeling, and allow yourself to recognize the preciousness of your loss.

Today

Know that you are *not* robbed of the ongoing love that still exists.

March 7

There is a new relationship unfolding between you and your loved one. It is based on memory, on spiritual presence, on dreams, on felt-sense, on LOVE. The relationship you knew, based on form, has re-formed into something different but equally powerful. Even as you continue to love them this change will unfold.

Today

Open yourself to the new relationship that is emerging, a relationship of spirit and love.

March 8

Grieving is exhausting work. Some days your energy is simply so heavy, so down, so weighted that you can barely get out of bed. Let the heaviness be. It won't always feel this intense, not every day; but for now, it does. Be gentle and permissive with yourself. Rest when you can.

Today

Give yourself permission to rest.

March 9

It is common for people to try to minimize your pain: "Oh but you had so many years together," "You're young," "You'll have other children," "You'll find someone else," "It was only a pet." People do this because they have such a hard time with pain (yours and/or theirs). Know that your pain is acceptable. You don't need to minimize it or hide it.

Today

Do not minimize the vastness of your pain, no matter what anyone else says.

March 10

Most people are terrified of dying. However, when you have a dear one who has already crossed over, death sometimes becomes less frightening. The sting of death has been taken away. In fact, it's typical to look forward to the time when you will be reunited with your dear ones. Just know that until that time comes there is a reason for you to still be here.

Today

Reflect on how your views of your own death are changing.

March 11

Grief is like a massive storm—a hurricane, a tsunami—that sweeps through your life, leaving destruction and devastation. You hold on tight but recognize that you cannot control the storm. However, you can reach out to others also affected by their own storms and begin to rebuild together.

Today

Call another griever today.

March 12

Let the photographs of your loved one be a testimony to a rich life filled with love and happy memories. Yes, images can sometimes cause a slice of pain as you remember what is lost. But be open to a shift whereby photos also remind you that each dear relationship is still a part of you, intrinsically woven into your heart and soul. These pictures honor life.

Today

Allow yourself a quiet time to look through some photographs of your loved one.

March 13

You might think that you're doing better and then suddenly dissolve into tears with virtually no warning. Perhaps a song, a smell, a memory triggers your sorrow. Know that no matter how many years have gone by, you will occasionally have these grief "bursts" that take your breath away. So intentionally breathe deeply and let it be. See each burst as another way to connect to your loved one.

Today

If grief bursts through, let it do so without your judgment.

March 14

It helps to believe that your dear ones are in a place of supreme beauty and intense divine love. Although you'd rather that they be with you, knowing they are so cared for can bring immeasurable comfort. Without this belief, grief can feel even more painful. Open your heart to the possibility of something else, and keep holding open that door of possibility.

Today

Be curious about the promise of something more, of mystery.

March 15

Grief is not something that you get over; you learn to live with and accommodate it. Love is also not something that you get over; you learn to let it shine through you. Your dear one is always with you, part of you, watching over you. Let the love that you were gifted radiate through you. This will make your grief more bearable.

Today

Let your dear one's love shine through you.

March 16

One of the mysteries of life is that you can have two opposing feelings be true at the same time. You can have sorrow even as you feel joy. You can have tears and laughter simultaneously. You can be grieving and grateful side by side. So look at what else you can hold next to your heartbreak and let it be.

Today

Know that both love and loss are true at the same time.

March 17

You are stronger than you know. Although you may feel fragile, weak, collapsed, it takes enormous strength and courage to feel your pain and do the work of grieving. Know that you are being supported by friends, strangers, and angels (both on earth and beyond). And, of course, your beloved dear one is offering you strength mixed with enduring love.

Today

Recognize the strength that it takes to endure profound grief.

March 18

You will most likely miss your beloved every single day . . . no matter how many years go by. There is nothing wrong or abnormal about this. It's part of loving, living, and losing. Notice the sadness and longing, but also notice the love that lives on through death that will always be a part of you.

Today

Know that it's okay to continue to miss your loved one.

March 19

The dream world is a place where many people experience visitations from their loved ones. Notice if you have dreams that feel shockingly real and clear. It can be upsetting to wake up and remember that your beloved isn't physically here. Shift your attention to the gift of the dream and know that your dear one was trying to connect with you.

Today

Ask your dear one to come visit you in a dream.

March 20

The process of grieving is not linear—it's more like a spiral. You feel as if you're going around in circles, but actually you are always coming around to a new dimension. You go deeper into the grief and also upward in a lift toward transcendence. Trust the process and be gentle with yourself on the journey.

Today

Know that your process is a spiral of growth.

March 21

As spring approaches, notice the new life that is coming to the earth. See the leaves, the fresh grass, the flower buds. Spring comes after the earth has been in a state of winter sleep. New things are possible, even when change seems impossible. Your grief can take you to places of new growth, new perspectives, new ways to engage with life. Let spring start to blossom in your heart.

Today

Even if you're not experiencing it yet, remember that winter eventually thaws to spring.

March 22

You know how much you've been changed because of your loved one's death, but consider how much you've been changed because of their life. Who were you before they entered your world? Who did they help you become? How are you different for having loved them? How are you different for having been loved? Hold these answers close to your heart.

Today

Think of three ways that you're different because of knowing and loving your dear one.

March 23

You have an angel watching over you. What would they say to you if they could whisper in your ear? What might they tell you about how you should live your days while you still have them? What would they want you to know about love? Perhaps they would tell you that love lasts for eternity and can never be diminished by death.

Today

Close your eyes and listen . . . can you hear a whisper?

March 24

We cannot avoid pain in this lifetime . . . loss, sickness, aging, death—these aspects of life are inevitable. We are all in the same boat: Pain is a certainty. However, suffering is optional. We have a choice to use pain as a means of learning, as a springboard for growth. We can transmute our pain into compassion, strength, and inspiration. While this transformation takes time, know that it is possible.

Today

Be open to transformation.

March 25

What is loss teaching you about life? Is it teaching you to be bitter and broken? Is it teaching you to be compassionate and vibrant? Perhaps it's teaching you about the complexity of a world where there is great sorrow, great love, *and* great mystery. Notice what you are learning and what you'd like to be learning.

Today

What have you already learned from loss?

March 26

A creative way to preserve beloved shirts, ties, dresses, pants, or nightgowns is to create a memory quilt. You can snuggle up with your dear one's old favorites rather than just storing them in a closet or giving them to charity. You can also make pillows with flannel shirts to accompany the quilt. Wrapping yourself in comfort made of their precious clothing is a wonderful way to stay connected.

Today

Do something creative with your loved one's clothes. Put the wheels in motion to create a quilt or pillow.

March 27

A life is pure and perfect no matter how many years it lasts. It is not for us to know how long a life "should" last. Nor is it for us to know the intricate meaning behind what looks senseless. Instead, we are left to pick up the pieces, to continue to love, to integrate loss into our being, and to create meaning out of the days we still have.

Today

Try not to judge the measure of a life by its length.

March 28

It can be tempting to cast blame for your current loss. Is there a person to bring to justice? Was a doctor at fault? Was someone else responsible for your misery? Pointing a finger, and even exacting vengeance, is a way of delaying your inevitable grief process. No matter what, it won't bring back your loved one. Anger is a slow poison that eats away within you.

Today

See if you can breathe in freedom from the desire to blame others.

March 29

If your anguished pain could be instantly erased, but it meant that you had never known your loved one, my guess is that you would keep your grief. This grief that challenges you is the price tag for loving your dear one. Grief is tolerable because love is eternal. The love is more powerful, more pervasive, more enduring, and more life changing than the pain.

Today

Remember that you would never erase the pain if it meant also erasing your relationship. Let the pain remind you of the blessing of loving your dear one.

March 30

How would your loved one be grieving if you had gone first?
Do you think that they would have suffered tremendously
over grieving you? Would they have crumbled or been an
inspiration? Have they been spared agonizing grief? What
can you learn by trying to imagine the tables turned?

Today

Consider whether your loved one has been spared the
agony of grief.

March 31

Sometimes, people are afraid of putting down their pain,
as if the agonizing sorrow is the only connection they
have to their loved one. Are you afraid that if you give up
the pain you will lose the relationship? While pain is part
of the process, living, loving, and embracing life are also
part of the process. Even when the pain starts to dimin-
ish, you are *still* connected. Pain is not your only tie to
your loved one.

Today

Be willing to let the pain go at times, guilt-free.

April 1

Know that you are more vast and expansive than your identity as a "griever." There is a part of you bigger than your experience, a part that is wiser, and in touch with the lessons of loss. If you could choose how you'd like to be on the journey with grief, what would you choose? To be strong? Compassionate? Peaceful? Full of love? Set your intention and start to become it, knowing that you have a wide spaciousness within.

Today

Look up to the sky. The spaciousness above mirrors the spaciousness within you.

April 2

You are still in a relationship with your dear one, regardless of how many years they have been "gone." You talk to them, look at their pictures, savor memories, talk about them, and maybe even journal to them. This is all normal. They are part of your history—part of the fabric of *you*. Remember that the relationship is still vibrant.

Today

Embrace the fact that you are still connected, now and forever.

April 3

Sometimes, you might be worried that you'll forget the details of your loved one—the sound of their voice, the twinkle in their eyes. Although some details will fade, it's true, do not be concerned. The essence of your dear one will be with you always. The core truth of them will never fade from your heart.

Today

Rest in the knowledge that the most essential aspects of your dear one will always be imprinted upon you.

April 4

There are certain times of the year, certain trigger days, that might feel extra raw for you. You can expect to be more sensitive, more prone to tears, more irritable. It could be a wedding anniversary, the time of diagnosis, a birthday, or the departure day. See these times as a chance to revisit your grief and deepen your attachment to your loved one. Use the time to give yourself permission to feel your pain and to honor their amazing impact on your life.

Today

You have permission to feel your pain in all its depth.

April 5

The ripple effect of our loved ones' lives is vast. They live on through you; they live on through the memories of others. Their lives and their deaths touched people in ways you cannot even imagine. Let their impact continue to be a positive one in the way that you use your grief and channel it into new pathways of life.

Today

How do you see your loved one living through you?

April 6

People will sometimes say words that come across as unkind. Words such as, "Get over it," or "When will you be your old self again?" Some so-called "friends" may even turn their backs on you. Know that they simply don't understand grief, nor have they walked in your shoes. Although you may feel angry, try to open your heart with compassion for those who just don't get it. One day, most likely, they will understand.

Today

Realize that when people say unintentionally hurtful words, they simply haven't experienced what you've experienced.

April 7

You are not alone in your grief. There are millions of people around the globe who understand your pain. Every country, every city, every town, every village has people in it who have loved and lost people dear to them. Grieving is part of the human condition and has been throughout all of time. Though you may feel alone, stop to remember that you are part of a vast network of people who are learning to live with loss and hold love gently in their hearts.

Today

Imagine grievers in every corner of the globe who share your experience and hold loss and love·in their hearts every day of their lives, just as you do.

April 8

When you are in deep grief, it is not unusual to want to leave this planet. You are feeling such overwhelming pain that living almost seems pointless. Know that other grievers feel this way, too. However, acting on this feeling is something else . . . hold on. Stay with the feeling, and then watch as it starts to shift and change. Life will begin to have meaning again in a new way. Observe your thoughts and wait until it is your time to transition.

Today

Accept the feeling of wanting to die but do not act upon it.

April 9

Grief is not something that you will get over, be cured of, or be done with—you can't stuff it in a box and throw it away. Instead, grief is something you will learn to live with. You will integrate it, synthesize it, and allow it to change you. The change will be subtle and not subtle simultaneously. Grief will influence your perspective on life and death, and on love itself. But know that love, like grief, will always be a part of you, too. Your soul is infused with the love of all the people who have left this earth before you. Happily, there is no end to that, either.

Today

Know that just as there is no closure on grief, there is no closure on love.

April 10

The second year of grieving is sometimes harder than the first year. Why? Because often, the first year is about integrating shock (especially if the loss is sudden and traumatic). In the second year, the shock begins to wear off and reality sets in. The pain sinks down to your roots. It's not uncommon to expect to feel significantly better after the first year "angelversary" and then to be depressed when you don't. Know that an increase in your grief is not unusual in the second year. The feelings will change and soften with time if you let yourself feel them.

Today

Let each year of grief be what it needs to be.

April 11

Grief takes you to places you never even knew existed. It asks you to dig deep into your heart and soul to discover what lies within. You will feel more pain than you thought possible, more disappointment than you can bear, and perhaps even more love than you realized. On other days, you may feel nothing at all but a dull numbness. Know that all of this is part of the ever-changing landscape of grief.

Today

Notice how the process of grief changes from day to day.

April 12

If people ask, "When will you be your old self again?" Say, "A new self is in the process of emerging." Grief changes you irrevocably in all sorts of ways. You might be less innocent, less trusting, or less free. But you might also be more compassionate, more wise, and more understanding. Watch as grief carves you into a new self. Every profound experience in life invites you to grow and shape-shift into a new you . . . or even, perhaps, into more of the real you.

Today

Who are you becoming as you live with loss?

April 13

Look around. Who is left in your life to love? What beloved person or pet is waiting for your attention, longing for your energy? Remember to savor the relationships that are still present on this planet, for they too are precious. Perhaps even now someone is craving a connection with you. Try to be open to love coming to you from multiple sources.

Today

Find ways to celebrate the living.

April 14

We are like sea glass as we grieve. We start with sharp, jagged edges as our world is shattered. And then, with time, with mourning, with sharing, with reaching out, with grieving some more, our edges get softened. When we let grief change us, we take on a new shape. Let yourself become softened by the sea of grief.

Today

Can you allow yourself to be a molded piece of sea glass?

April 15

It is normal to miss your dear one with a fierce intensity. You will miss their voice, their touch, their laughter, their perspective, their humor, their stories, their mannerisms, their smile. At times, it will hurt so much that you'll wonder whether you'll ever survive it. And then, when you do survive it, you'll wish that you hadn't. Hang on, my friend. Grieving is some of the hardest emotional work you'll ever have to do.

Today

Breathe into the sorrow of missing your dear one.

April 16

It's easy to believe that you don't have anything for which to be grateful when you're in the midst of heartbreaking grief. But look closer—notice the tiny details to be thankful for: electricity, a warm bed, good food, friends who care, online communities, pets, living in a country you cherish, running water, flowers, frost, sunshine. Most of all, know that the love and essence of your beloved will *always* be with you, *always* be a part of your life. For that, you can be especially grateful.

Today

List three things in your life for which you are grateful.

April 17

While we often think there are "bad" days and "better" days, they are all simply days on the journey. Some days are saturated with grief, in which the energy is heavy and sorrowful. Other days have a little more light, gratitude, and peace. Each type of day is necessary on this journey.

Today

Let the day be what it needs to be.

April 18

Each person in your life, each relationship, is completely unique and irreplaceable. You can move forward with new people and new relationships, but they will never replace the old. If you're a widow and you get remarried, if you're a bereaved parent and have another baby, yes, there is joy in the new. However, your grief is not erased; your old love is still there. Fortunately, the human heart expands to accommodate all of our many loves and relationships. Just remember that no life is replaced or forgotten.

Today

Know that every single loved one in your life is special in their own way.

April 19

You probably didn't expect grief to hurt so much—or expect that you could endure such intense pain. You probably didn't expect to become a different person after this loss. And wasn't it a shock that grief doesn't end, it simply changes? But perhaps most surprising of all, isn't it amazing that love is a bridge to keep you forever connected to your loved one, even in spite of death?

Today

What did you expect about grief?

April 20

What you are feeling today is for *today* only. You just need to feel it now. Whether you can look at a photo today or not, whether you cry in the shower today or not, whether you smile today or not, just be with it today. Tomorrow or the next day or next year will be different. In fact, you don't know precisely how your grief will look or feel then. All you know is what it is like today.

Today

Don't worry about what you will feel down the road. Just focus on what you're feeling today.

April 21

Your loved one has transformed and gone on to some-place we can barely imagine. You too are in the process of transforming, unfolding into a different version of yourself. Be open to the process of growth and newness, watching with curiosity as wings unfold. Know that it's because of your relationship with your loved one that you are who you are. And it's because of transformation that you're becoming who you are becoming.

Today

Open yourself to transformation, carved by love and by grief.

April 22

What would your life be like if you had never known your beloved? You would have none of your current grief or sorrow. You would be spared the suffering you endure today. But you would also never have known that pro-found love. You would be a different you. The trajectory of your life would be unrecognizable.

Today

Be filled with awe that your loved one came to grace your life, for however long.

April 23

Your loved one is always a part of you. Therefore, when you "move forward" (as opposed to "move on"), you take them with you. They are never more than a heartbeat away. They infuse your every breath with their love and their influence in your life. So take a step forward without guilt, knowing that when you reengage with life, they are forever with you.

Today

Accept that as you move forward, your loved one will always be with you.

April 24

You never have to apologize for tears. Whether your eyes are merely misty or you could fill the ocean with your outpouring, tears are an expression of true emotion. They cleanse you, moving emotion through your body. Whether you cry in public or in private, let the tears flow without self-judgment.

Today

Know that tears offer emotional and physical cleansing.

April 25

No matter how many years go by, the sadness of grief will at times be in the background. What, however, is in the foreground? Grief will have a tendency to come to the front, becoming your sole focus, pushing love and beautiful memories into the background. Experiment with shifting your focus so that love is front and center.

Today

Can you keep love in the foreground of your mind?

April 26

Deciding to stay engaged with life, and with those still on this planet, is a daily choice. I believe that your loved ones would want you to make that choice. They know there is still a reason for you to be here, and they are waiting patiently for your reunion. Choose life. Yes, life is often heartbreaking, ugly, harsh, and painful. But it is also touching, beautiful, and glorious. Remember that with every step, you are supported and loved.

Today

Make a decision to choose life and love in spite of loss.

April 27

There will be days when you simply do not know how you will survive. You cannot imagine a future without your dear one, and you cannot imagine a present day without unbearable pain. Just focus on your breath, in this moment. Every morning that you wake up, you are surviving. Keep choosing to survive, and the days will eventually get easier.

Today

Affirm that today you are a survivor.

April 28

Relationships have three primary components: physical, emotional, and spiritual. When a loved one dies, we lose the physical aspect to the relationship. It is natural to desperately miss their form and to long for it. Fortunately, the emotional and spiritual sides of our relationships are very much alive even when the physical form has left. Remember that you still have two out of three aspects of your relationship with your loved one.

Today

Focus on the elements of your relationship that are still vibrant.

April 29

Strength—people say that you're strong, but you don't always feel it. Strength is often confused with a sort of stoicism, a pull-yourself-up-by-the-bootstraps mentality. What people don't realize is that it takes an enormous amount of strength to actually face grief, to cry and fall apart and turn within. It also takes strength to keep functioning in this world when you'd rather not. Know that strength comes from within you but also from beyond you (from your loved one who has passed, from your loved ones who are still here, and from divine energy). You are stronger than you realize.

Today

Do you know that you are strong, even when you feel weak?

April 30

It can be especially painful to not be able to call your loved one (or email them, text them, etc.) You may have had regular get-togethers or phone dates, maybe daily, weekly, or monthly. Now, the time when you would have communicated comes and goes, and your heart breaks. Know that while communication with your loved one has changed forever, there are still ways to connect. The bond continues.

Today

Write a letter to your dear one.

May 1

If you don't start to process your grief (talk about it, cry about it, let it change you in new ways), then your grief will stay hidden. You may think you've outwitted it, but in fact it is there behind a wall, making you sick and shutting down your life. Feeling grief is part of living. Know that your pain has a purpose.

Today

Have you been suppressing your grief?

May 2

I often hear, "I thought I'd be better by now." Remember that grief is not something that you get over, but something that you integrate into your life. Both loss and love are inextricably entwined into your being. Some days this integration will feel possible and some days it will feel impossible. Breathe into it and hold all of the feelings in your heart, without judgment.

Today

Remember that grief is a lifelong process of integration.

May 3

Have compassion for yourself. Grieving is an enormous emotional, physical, and spiritual undertaking. Let yourself rest when you need to, cry when you need to, withdraw when you need to, reach out when you need to. Wrap yourself in tender understanding as you release all self-criticism and judgment.

Today

Be with your experience exactly as it is.

May 4

Do you ever feel guilty for enjoying a wonderful moment? Remember that you're still on this planet to live and to grow. When you savor life, you honor your loved one. Learning to live—in spite of pain, in spite of loss—is a tribute to the love that your dear one imparts to you.

Today

Let the guilt go.

May 5

Going through the closets and possessions of a loved one can feel like an overwhelming, endless task. Sorting, giving, keeping, disposing, all the while feeling your emotions come over you like a lead blanket. Take your time with this process, chunking it into small tasks when possible. Get the assistance of friends or family if you can. Remember that you may give away the possessions of your loved one, but that in no way diminishes your connection to them.

Today

Know that when you give your loved one's things away, you create a cycle of generosity.

May 6

The question "Why?" can be haunting. Why did they have to die? Why did they suffer? Why did this happen? The painful question of "Why?" may never have an answer that we can understand in this lifetime. Put down your quest to know why, and instead turn your attention to the question, "What now?" As you tolerate uncertainty and live into the question, bit by bit, of "What now?" your energy will shift.

Today

Begin to open up to the possibility of living into the unknown.

May 7

Although special trigger days (a birthday, an anniversary) can be especially emotional, it could also be any ordinary Tuesday that takes your breath away. Grief will sneak up on you . . . there doesn't have to be a reason for you to feel your feelings. Grief has a way of showing up (a song on the radio, a comment, a photo). Just let the feelings pass through you, without judgment. It is the way of the grief journey.

Today

Let your feelings arise and fall away.

May 8

Think of people around the globe who are mourning.
Mothers, wives, husbands, sisters, sons, fathers . . . all
feeling the intense pain that grief brings. Think too of
all the profound love that fuels such loss. Have compassion for all the people living with their grief and then
turn that compassion toward yourself. You are part of the
human experience.

Today

Know that you are connected to all beings who know both
love and loss.

May 9

Look back over your grief journey, whether it has been weeks or years. You may think that your grief hasn't changed at all, but it has. Think back to subtle changes, to when you cried more or less, slept more or less, talked to others more or less. Reread old journals (if you have them), and look at how the journey has taken you up and down, around and back again. Grief is always moving. You've come farther than you may have realized . . . and the journey continues.

Today

Notice the subtle shifts that have occurred in your grief over time.

May 10

Your grief, your loss, is a piece to the puzzle of your life. It is not your *whole* life. It is a significant piece, yes, but take time to notice all the pieces in the puzzle. Your life is bigger than your loss. All the pieces are important.

Today

Name five other pieces to the puzzle of your life besides your grief.

May 11

When you grieve, you may fear that letting yourself go into the pain is like falling into a pit, a pit you may not be able to get out of. And so you avoid, suppress, deny. It is natural to fear that if you start crying, the tears will never end or to fear that you'll sink into an abyss with no way out. But tears do eventually stop. There is a way out of the abyss.

Today

Remember that your grief is not quicksand; it's a natural process in response to loss.

May 12

Loss and love always go hand in hand. We feel the pain of loss because we love. And when we love, we will eventually lose the physical form (our loved one's and our own). However, we never actually lose the love. The love is with us when we move forward into life. The love is with us in our hearts when we laugh, when we cry. The love is part of our very essence.

Today

Remember that true love never dies.

May 13

It's natural to have a place, a corner, or a "shrine" filled
with objects that remind you of your loved one. Although
many non-grievers are uncomfortable with this concept,
it is perfectly natural. It can bring comfort to create such
a place—a shelf, a corner that is filled with symbols of
your love for and connection to this person. Let it be a
place of honoring, a place that fortifies you to carry their
love with you as you keep living.

Today

Create (or add to) a corner with special objects dedicated
to your dear one.

May 14

Although their physical form is gone, you are not living your life without your loved one. To live truly without them would be never to have known them, ever. Instead, you continue to live with them infused in your heart, in your memories, in your spirit. You live with their love etched into your being. The you without them today is not the same as the you who never knew them.

Today

Remember that your dear one is with you in spirit, in memory, in your heart, and in your soul.

May 15

It can be painful to be surrounded by people who don't understand grief. They don't mean to be unkind, but they often make unhelpful comments. That's why support groups and online forums make such a difference on the journey. Connecting with people who understand, who have similar experiences, who "know" is extremely healing. Remember how much you help each other.

Today

Reach out to another griever.

May 16

Every single soul is unique and irreplaceable. So, when you lose someone (whether it's a stillborn child, someone you've known for many years, or even a pet), no other being can ever take their place. Even if you have other children, other siblings, another spouse, other pets, no one duplicates that singular relationship. Honor each relationship and its own miraculous place in your life.

Today

Hold close to your heart the unique treasure of each irreplaceable relationship.

May 17

You do not need to know how things will unfold over time. You do not need to know what will be happening next year or how you will get there. You just need to get up today and do the next right thing. Focus on this day, being with the simplicity of each moment, and you will gradually live your way into the future.

Today

Allow yourself to feel your feet on the floor as you sit and as you walk. Be aware of how the ground supports you with each step.

May 18

Do you notice your grief turning to compassion? Not only compassion for other grievers, but for all those who suffer? Let your grief carve within your heart a place that understands human suffering on a different level. Don't forget to turn that compassion toward yourself as well. From great pain can come great compassion.

Today

Reach out to someone in pain.

May 19

Grief is like a roller coaster. You think you are catching your breath, and then you plummet again. It takes you up, down, around and around again. The twists and turns are exhausting. Know that the intensity of the ride will change over time, taking you to new places. Hold on and remember to breathe.

Today

Breathe in for the count of five. Hold for the count of five. Exhale for the count of five. Repeat.

May 20

There is a longing for your loved one that simply takes your breath away. The yearning touches you physically, emotionally, and spiritually. This intense longing is normal, and you are not alone in experiencing it. Watch this feeling, and keep reminding yourself that you can focus on it exclusively, or you can bring your attention back to how your life is enriched because of your profound love.

Today

When your longing overwhelms you, remember to breathe in love.

May 21

It can be quite therapeutic to write. You can keep a grief journal in which you record your feelings, dialogue with grief, and share all the complex feelings in your heart. You can also keep a log of letters that you write to your beloved, sharing what's going on, how you miss them, and what you wish to tell them. Writing offers a release of emotion. With an open heart, try journaling or letter writing, or both, and see how it feels.

Today

Write down your feelings of grief. It helps to dilute the feelings of overwhelm.

May 22

Sometimes, the tragedy of death, or the pain of the final days, can loom large in your memory. Remember that your loved one was so much more than the way they passed. Remember the way they lived and the way they loved . . . keep the broader picture in mind. Don't let the manner of their death be the only part of their life that occupies your mind.

Today

Affirm that your dear one's life is larger than their death.

May 23

Grief is a teacher in our lives . . . it teaches us about life, about death, about love, about living, about patience, and about self-compassion. Although you didn't invite this teacher into your life, it is here nonetheless.

Today

What are you learning on this painful, life-changing journey?

May 24

The veil between this world and the next is quite thin. Frequently, if we are open to it, we can receive signs from our loved ones who have passed. Signs can come through nature, through electricity (lights turning on or off), through dreams, through songs, through other people. Receive each sign as a gift, as a token of enduring love.

Today

Are you open to receiving a sign from your loved one?

May 25

When you wake in the morning, the shock of remembering your loss can make your stomach sink. You remember all over again, *Oh yes, they're gone.* You might find that a heaviness or sorrow descends upon you as you emerge from sleep. Try pairing your realization with another feeling: cherished love. Remember that eternal love is like a light in the darkness.

Today

Imagine something that your loved one would say or do.

May 26

Your grief is like the ocean; emotions will crash upon you and then recede. Your feelings will ebb and flow. Just when you think you are clear, another wave will come over you. Watch, for the waves will begin to space themselves out . . . the intense ones will come less frequently. Observe the natural rhythm, and don't fight the waves.

Today

Let the waves of grief wash over you without any resistance.

May 27

Fear of death and dying is the number one human fear. Many people spend their lives terrified of the idea. Yet, once you have lost a beloved dear one, death loses its sting. In fact, grievers often look forward to death as a heavenly reunion with special souls. Watch how fear of death begins to lose its power in your life.

Today

Know that when the time is right, you too will transition to another dimension. When that happens, you will have a wonderful, blessed reunion.

May 28

With the grieving process, it may feel as if you are going around in circles. You keep coming back around to feelings that you thought you had finished. And yet, there you are back at the same feeling again. However it may appear, each time you come around is a new and different experience. You have spiraled to a slightly different plane, going higher and reaching deeper. So even as it seems to come back upon itself, the path of grief moves vertically. When you feel like you're back full circle, you have arrived at a new level in the process.

Today

Know that you are growing, even if it feels like you're back at the same place.

May 29

What "legacy" has your dear one left to you? Is it to carry on a dream? To dwell in peace and love? To struggle with an illness or carry on a grudge? How do you want their legacy to unfold? Think of their life, what they inspired in you and in others. Think about how to carry on with that inspiration.

Today

Imagine how your dear one would wish you to live in their honor.

May 30

Grief can make you feel like you're going crazy—losing things, having trouble concentrating. Remember that grief is a normal response to loss. You are not going crazy; you are simply feeling the response of loving someone and having them leave the planet before you. Feeling the impact authentically is not crazy.

Today

Remember that you are not going insane. You are grieving.

May 31

Never be reluctant to mention your loved one. Often,
friends don't realize that you welcome their memories.
They might be afraid to refer to your loved one because it
might upset you (as if you aren't already upset and thinking about them). They don't realize that mentioning your
loved one is a gift to you. Help them understand that it's
healthy to remember and honor your loved one. Consider
yourself an educator, and lead by example.

Today

Share a beloved memory of your dear loved one.

June 1

You are forever changed as a result of your profound loss. The answer to the question, "When will you be your old self again?" is "Never." You are a new self, a self who has been deeply touched by loss. But do not forget that you have been deeply touched by love as well. We are all beings who evolve and grow based on our life (and loss) experiences.

Today

Let your new self emerge as a person profoundly touched by love.

June 2

Separation is an illusion. Though your loved one is not physically with you, they are with you spiritually and energetically. They live in you and through you. They are ever with you, as close as your breath. When you are overwhelmed with missing their form, remember that their essence is woven into the fabric of you, now and forever.

Today

Close your eyes and feel your loved one near you.

June 3

Your task is not to let go. You need never let go. Why? Because your dear one will always be a part of you, intricately part of your mind and soul. Instead, your task is to carry your dear one into every part of your life. Let them energize your time remaining on the planet.

Today

Choose to move on *with* your loved one in your heart.

June 4

Every single soul is unique. So, when you lose someone (whether an infant, someone you've known for many years, or even a pet), no other being can ever take their place. Even if you have other children, other animals, other siblings, or eventually another spouse, no one duplicates that singular relationship. Honor each relationship as its own miraculous place in your life.

Today

Hold close to your heart the special treasure of each irreplaceable relationship.

June 5

Does pain ease over time? For many, the intense, sharp pain starts to space out, coming in intervals that are less frequent. For others, the pain transforms into a new perspective, a new intensity for living. And for others still, the pain is like an ongoing vice grip. One thing is for sure: Loss is part of your life now. How that will impact your life is partially up to you. Over time, you will have choices about how to integrate love and loss and how to focus your perspective. Let yourself grieve, and you will live more fully into the choices.

Today

Remember that you have choices about how grief will transform your life.

June 6

Grief is an invisible wound. You know that you are hurting and suffering, but you mostly look "just fine." You go through the motions of living—you show up for work, pay the bills, feed the pets, get up the next day. People might even praise you for "doing so well." What they may not realize is that you are broken inside, torn asunder. But know that healing will start to happen, bit by bit.

Today

Pay attention to what is going on inside you, underneath everything that looks "fine."

June 7

It's easy to think of grief as the enemy, the invader. However, it's also possible to face grief with curiosity. Grief is your companion now, a live-in guide who will decorate the foreground and the background of your life. Fortunately, your loved one is also a constant companion, whose love is always with you . . . as near as your next breath.

Today

Can you make friends with grief . . . or at least invite the uninvited guest in for a cup of tea?

June 8

There is a difference between a broken heart and a heart broken open. The broken heart is jagged and leads to shutting down on life. The heart broken open creates the possibility for light to filter in. In that open space, there is room for compassion and tenderness to grow. In the end, choice helps to shape your experience. Choose to let your heart be broken open, and see what remains to grow.

Today

What is there room for in your heart broken open?

June 9

There are mysteries in this life, things we cannot know or understand or explain. Rest in the not-knowing. Watch how nature quiets life in the winter only to revive life in the spring. We only see a small part in the vast chain of life and death. One thing we are sure about is that love is deep, vast, and eternal.

Today

Begin to tolerate the reality that there is much we cannot know or understand in this life.

June 10

We are a grief-averse culture. We go to extreme measures to avoid feeling pain. It can be tempting to drown our sorrows in alcohol or distract ourselves with eating, shopping, gambling, or excessive screen time. There's nothing inherently wrong with wanting to avoid pain. Pain *is* painful. It's also important, however, to face the pain, since in that experience is the path of healing.

Today

Choose a path of moderation and balance: Face pain and also take a break from it.

June 11

Some days will feel like "bad" days, and some days will feel like "good" days. Or maybe they all feel "bad" right now. Know that they are all days for you to grieve, to love, to ride the ridges of grief, and to keep growing through this process. No matter what, know that every day you have been touched and changed by love. Nothing will change that, not even death.

Today

Accept the day as it comes, whatever might arise.

June 12

You have permission to actively seek comfort today. Ask for and receive a hug. Cuddle with a teddy bear. Take a soothing bath. Drink tea. Listen to music. Cry with a friend. Write in a journal. Walk in the woods. Play with your cat. Look at beautiful photographs online. Find something today to bring comfort to your weary, sad self. When you are grieving, you deserve to experience both large and small moments of daily comfort.

Today

Find some comfort today—you deserve it.

June 13

What if you and your loved one were estranged? What if you had conflicts on a regular basis? What if you even had an argument shortly before they died? Relationships are complicated because we are all complex individuals. You can love someone and still be annoyed by them. Don't punish yourself for being human. Whatever happened is over now, forgiven. Now it's time to forgive yourself.

Today

Remember that love is big enough to embrace even our foibles.

June 14

Some days you simply do not know how you are going to get through this, how you are going to live one more day. That's when you need to focus on this hour, this minute, just getting through . . . one second at a time. There is a reason you are still here, even if you are unaware of that reason right now. So breathe deeply, and remember that others know the pain of loss, share it, and are getting through one more day just like you are.

Today

Breathe into this one moment. Be with it fully.

June 15

Time alone does not heal all wounds. But time plus the willingness to feel and express your pain does begin a healing process that continues over time. Even if you face your grief head-on early in the process, there will always be some sadness over time, though the sharpness will soften. When you don't give yourself permission to grieve, time will simply hide a deep and aching wound, which will permeate your life.

Today

Know that facing your grief is the healthy choice for healing. Then time will be on your side.

June 16

Notice if aspects of your dear one are expressing themselves through you. Maybe you tell your mom's jokes, make your wife's cookie recipe, sing your daughter's favorite songs. Or maybe you begin to see life as if through their lens. Let parts of them flow through you. Welcome the assimilation. It's another way to stay connected to them, full of love.

Today

What cherished part of your loved one could you take on as part of you?

June 17

There is a new normal in your life now. Without your loved one's physical presence, your world looks slightly different. And whatever it is today, it will be different as time passes. Rather than curse the new reality, try opening to it with a gentle curiosity. Remember that your loved one is a heartbeat away as you navigate this new terrain.

Today

Put your hand over your heart and be curious about how the new normal is going to look in your life.

June 18

For many grievers, the first year (maybe even longer) is a complete blur. A combination of shock, adaptation, and incomprehensible overwhelm make life feel like a dream. This is quite normal. Know that the spirit begins to adjust, and life will come into focus again one day. Your perspective will be different, and in some places even clearer. The blur, however, is typical in the beginning.

Today

If you are in the first year of your grieving, know that it's typical for life to be like a fuzzy, bad dream.

June 19

You are a survivor. Every day that you get through, every task that you accomplish, every breath that you take . . . you are surviving. So what gives you the resilience? It could be that you must remain strong for other people on this planet. Or you have tapped into your core strength. Perhaps your faith or your connection to nature gives you strength. Or maybe it's your sense of mission. Dig deep inside—your strength is there.

Today

Name three things that help you survive (people, pets, places, spiritual experiences).

June 20

When a life ends, it seems like the light in the world gets a little dimmer. Remember that your dear one's light continues to shine through you in your memories. Let their love for you inspire you to be a beacon of love and light for others. The light is still there; it is just transformed.

Today

Close your eyes and let your loved one's light fill you, expand inside you, and emanate from within you.

June 21

Where do you most feel the presence of your dear one? Is it when you walk in the woods, when you hear a song, when you visit the cemetery, when you look at their photograph? Notice when and where this feeling arises. Though awareness can be painful, in truth it is a gift that keeps you connected. And if you are not feeling their presence at this time, be still . . . be quiet . . . be patient . . . be open to receiving.

Today

Can you feel the presence of your loved one?

June 22

C. S. Lewis, the beloved author who lost his wife to cancer, once said, "The pain now is part of the happiness then." It does seem to be true that we suffer in our losses because the love and beauty were so dear. And yet, we would never give up that love in order to be spared the pain. If the price of love is pain, wouldn't you still pay?

Today

Would you give up the pain if it meant you had never known the happiness?

June 23

Your process is your own. You will not grieve exactly as anyone else. Therefore, be gentle with yourself. Perhaps you don't cry as much as your spouse or your sibling or your child . . . or perhaps you cry more. Maybe you want to share memories frequently . . . or maybe you don't. You are doing grief your way, at your pace. You have permission to do what feels natural to you and not grieve according to anyone else's plan.

Today

Honor the unique ways that you express your grief.

June 24

Be where you are today. Whether you are feeling extreme sorrow, anger, sadness, or even tiny flashes of happiness, be with your present state. Observe each feeling with curiosity and compassion. You will not feel this feeling exactly the same way tomorrow or a year from now. It is how you feel today, right now. Let it be, with tenderness.

Today

Be in this moment and allow it to be what it already is.

June 25

Grievers are there for each other. A certain magical connection is woven between and amongst people who understand and have known deep sorrow. You can feel it in grief groups. You can feel it in online communities. This connection is a healing balm. Know that as you reach out to another in pain, you are both healing. And as you receive love from another griever, you are both growing.

Today

Reach out to another griever today.

June 26

No matter what growth or meaning has occurred because of your loss, no matter how you have reengaged with life and love, there will still be days that bring you to your knees with grief. This is simply the nature of profound loss. Do not be alarmed when it happens . . . let it pass and allow a new day to dawn. And remember that while loss is your constant companion, so is love—now and forever.

Today

Expect grief to feel raw sometimes, even after many years.

June 27

Though your heart is broken, who else around you needs your love and attention? It could be a family member, a friend, a pet, a colleague, even a stranger . . . or perhaps yourself. Look around you at those beings still on the planet and see who needs your presence. You will always hold in your heart those who are dear to you, and your energy is important for someone still here.

Today

Turn your attention to a loved one still here, someone who needs your love.

June 28

Resilience refers to one's ability to cope with adversity. The human spirit is naturally quite resilient. Although you may be feeling exhausted, weak, and broken, those experiences are actually a form of strength. Letting yourself grieve takes tremendous courage. And then . . . you keep getting up and doing what needs to be done.

Today

Try thinking of yourself as resilient, knowing that contained in that word is the entire up-and-down process of living with loss.

June 29

You just don't know where grief is going to lead you. At the very least, it will introduce you to new people and to a deeper compassion for emotional pain. Think of those you have met because of your loss. True, you would always rather have your loved one back, but be open to where the path of grieving will take you and whose path you will cross because of it.

Today

Thank a friend for their understanding, someone you met because of your grief.

June 30

Some days the missing and the longing are just overwhelming. You can try to focus on the love, on the ongoing connection, but sometimes it just doesn't feel like enough. Let yourself be with the missing. You are entitled to miss their smile, their laugh, their humor, their stories. Part of being human is reacting to loss. Let yourself be human.

Today

Remember that grief is a natural reaction to loss.

July 1

Often, well-meaning people will ask, "Isn't it time that you move on?" Tell them that you will move forward when you are ready. And when you do, you will always have your dear one in your heart, woven into your soul, and within every breath.

Today

In what ways are you moving forward *with* your dear one?

July 2

Pain is a part of life, a natural and inevitable experience. Emotional pain can lead you to new places. Rather than resisting it, let it guide you and open you to a deeper experience of living. Embedded in the pain is always a deep love, which is a rich and abiding lifeline.

Today

Do not be afraid of your pain. It is a necessary part of the journey.

July 3

It can be difficult when others around you are excited to celebrate when you just feel like pulling the covers over your head. Holidays can ignite a feeling of being separate and different from others. Just anticipating a holiday is sometimes worse than the actual day. Listen within to what your mind and body need. Do they need rest or socializing? You have permission to do whatever works for you.

Today

Know that anticipating a holiday takes a great deal of emotional energy.

July 4

The United States celebrates Independence Day today, but we know that no one is truly independent. We are each *inter*dependent on the ones we love—both those currently on this planet and those who have departed. Take care today to let yourself feel connected without any self-judgment.

Today

Recognize that even now, you are interdependent with your beloved one.

July 5

Do you have someone to cry with? Tears shared can be particularly healing. Perhaps you cry with a family member, with a dear friend, with other grievers in a group. Or perhaps you share your tears via cyberspace. While sometimes it feels easier to cry alone, crying with another has a way of connecting you in a deep and intimate space.

Today

Don't be afraid to share your tears with another person.

July 6

Do you ever feel guilty for enjoying a wonderful moment? Remember that you're still on this planet to live and to grow. When you savor life, you honor your loved one. Learning to live—in spite of pain, in spite of loss—is a tribute to the love that your dear one imparts to you.

Today

Allow yourself to have a moment of happiness, in honor of your dear one.

July 7

Your dear one's life made a huge impact . . . how their love touched you, changed you . . . how their life touched others . . . how their death touched others. Know the ripple effect of their life continues to move through you and how you continue to live.

Today

Notice one way that your loved one lives on through you.

July 8

You will likely never know why your loved one died when they did. You may not know who you are becoming . . . yet. You may not know when you'll start to feel better. You may not even know how you'll get through this. But what you do know is that you loved someone deeply and that love continues through time and space. You do know that you are enriched by that love, which will forever be etched into your heart.

Today

Hold on to what you do know, and let the rest drift away like a passing cloud across the sky.

July 9

Sometimes, you might skate along the surface of your grief. It is there below as you move over it. And other times, you drop deep into the depths of the abyss that is grief. There, you touch the center of your pain. Both places are important aspects of your process. Both have their place.

Today

Accept where you are today, whether you're on the surface or deep down with your grief.

July 10

Try dosing your pain a little at a time . . . Write in a grief journal for ten minutes and then stop. Let yourself cry for five minutes in the shower and then stop. Think of this as taking grief in small, intentional, contained doses. Pain needs to be felt and expressed before it can circulate, but it can also be overwhelming unless you break it down.

Today

See if dosing the pain in smaller chunks helps you manage the feelings of grief.

July 11

Do not doubt that love is eternal. Love is a rich, deep, all-encompassing experience that cannot be erased by death. Love is a part of you now and always, suffused into your heart. The love you feel for and from your loved one is as close as your own heartbeat.

Today

Can you feel love beating in your heart?

July 12

For some people, the second year after a major loss is even more profoundly painful than the first. The reason for this is that the fog and blur of the first year have started to lift. Deep and intense pain reveals itself. Do not be afraid if this happens to you. Continue to ride the cycles of grief, and let the process unfold as it needs to.

Today

Be open to each year bringing its own challenges and gifts.

July 13

Have you *lost* your loved one? Yes . . . and no. Yes, you've lost their physical presence and their warm hugs around you. You've lost life on the planet with them. However, we are so much more than mere form. You have not lost their love, the impact of their life, their place in your heart. You have not lost your treasured past or everything that they are to you. You have not lost the fact that you're still in a relationship.

Today

Focus on what you still have and not just on what you've lost.

July 14

Part of the goal of living with loss is allowing yourself
to be connected to *all* of the dear ones who have left this
planet before you, the many loved ones who have passed
on. And one day, you will follow those who have paved
the way. You are part of a chain of people on this earth
who live, love, and leave. One day there will be people left
behind who light a candle in your memory.

Today

Hold in your heart the truth that you are part of a vast
web of human history.

July 15

Endings always have beginnings embedded within them. Although you would never have chosen these new beginnings, notice what has emerged out of your grief. Do you have new "grief friends" and connections? Do you have a different understanding of life and death and love? Do you have a new mission? Do you have new insights, or perhaps a new perspective on yourself?

Today

Look for the beginnings that have sprung from the endings in your life.

July 16

Although sorrow is a daily companion, so is love. Notice how love has changed you. Notice how the act of loving someone who is no longer physically here continues to change you. Keep your heart open to love and let it shine through you. That gift is part of their legacy.

Today

Love will continue to create change, if you let it into your heart.

July 17

When you experience a major loss, it's like the rug has been pulled out from under you. You fall hard, the wind knocked out of you. Everything looks different, sounds different, *is* different. Nothing is quite the same anymore.

Today

Stop. Breathe. Be patient with yourself as you begin to adjust to this new life.

July 18

There was a time when grievers were advised to cut their ties to the deceased. The psychological task of mourning was to let go. Now we know that the relationship you have with your dear ones is *not* over. Just because their form is no longer on the planet doesn't mean that your connection is severed. You will continue to love them, to talk to them, to write to them, to kiss their photo, and even (sometimes) to receive signs from them.

Today

Relish your continuing bonds.

July 19

Part of finding your bridge back to life is recognizing that you take your loved one with you everywhere you go. And you will take your loss with you as well. Love and loss are with you now and always, side by side. You can still make the choice to live, to savor the life left to you, and touch people with your heart and soul.

Today

Cross the bridge to your new life, holding love and loss together.

July 20

As you grieve, think about how you were taught to mourn when you were a child. Did you have an occasion to learn about loss then? Were healthy skills offered or not? Think back and recall what comforted you then. Use the past as an example of how to cope (or how not to).

Today

Notice what you can learn from the past.

July 21

Don't be afraid to talk about your dear ones who have died. Share stories; recall details. Many people will seem uncomfortable if you talk about the deceased. However, you can model it for those who are willing to participate. Also, find the people in your life who are easily able to talk and listen. It is a gift to share the memories.

Today

Share a story today to a receptive listener.

July 22

Is it possible that your loved one is watching over you, looking out for you, acting as an angel? Consider that they have your back as you keep living and growing and using your time left on the planet.

Today

Imagine your loved one supporting you from the other side of the veil.

July 23

Two things can be true simultaneously: You can be heart-broken and bereft, and you can be filled with gratitude for the amazing love that was in your life (and still is in your life, actually). Sorrow and joy exist side by side. Both are true and both are real.

Today

Wisdom is making space to hold two opposing truths at the same time.

July 24

Objects that belonged to your loved one can create a sense of continuation for you. Do you have something that they treasured? Perhaps a gift that they selected for you? Use a tangible item to remind you of their presence.

Today

Use an object to link you to your dear one's love.

July 25

Give yourself permission to do nothing. When you're grieving, your energy goes inward and it's hard to be productive. Our society wants you to *do*, but grief wants you to *be*. There will come a time when energy returns; but for now, whenever possible, be still.

Today

When you can, sit with no purpose other than to just be in stillness.

July 26

Sometimes, we put grief off for a while. Perhaps, at the time of the loss, we were overwhelmed. Perhaps we had to rally for some other situation. The thing about grief is that it waits for us. Even if it has been many years since the loss, you will be able to summon the feelings as if the loss had just occurred. It is never too late to do grief work. Facing your grief now will open you to a wider range of expressive feelings.

Today

Do you have some unprocessed grief from the past that needs your attention?

July 27

You may have lost more than one dear one . . . and if you live long enough, you are certain to lose many loved ones. Know that just as each relationship is unique, your grief for each is also unique. Focus on how each special love has molded you, influenced you, and formed you into the person you are today.

Today

Your grief for each relationship will be as unique as the relationships themselves.

July 28

It's natural to be concerned that you might forget details: the sound of their laughter, the gleam in their eye, the smell of their hair. Although some details do fade over time, the essence of them is forever etched clearly into your heart and spirit. You cannot lose what is most essential in their soul, for it is entwined within your own.

Today

Know that you will never lose or forget the essence of your loved one.

July 29

Grief has the potential to shut you down, making you bitter and cynical. Grief also has the potential to carve you into a wiser, more compassionate person. The direction in which you turn is largely your own choice. Even if you cannot make the choice for growth at this time, you can start to see it as an eventual goal.

Today

Choose the path of growth . . . now or as a possibility for the future.

July 30

Remember the life and love that touched you, enriched you, blessed you, and changed you. Their life is so much bigger than their death. If you are struggling with images of a painful, prolonged, or traumatic and sudden end, keep turning your attention to the life that made your life brighter and sweeter. Life and love are always bigger than death.

Today

Remember that your dear one's life is brighter than their death.

July 31

It's not unusual to wish to die, to go on to the next realm to be with your loved one. However, you are still on this planet because there is a reason for you to be here. While initially life feels like a process of waiting to die, gradually, bit by bit, start looking for ways to be here on purpose.

Today

Live in honor of your loved one.

August 1

Grief is like a spiral. You feel like you are going around in circles and coming back to the same material. But in fact, your grief is always in motion. This means that you come back to what seem like old feelings at a slightly different place on the path. You are changing, integrating, grieving, moving deeper, moving higher, always along the turns of this grief spiral. Be patient with yourself in the process.

Today

Know that grief is not a linear process, but rather a spiral journey.

August 2

Emotions are like water: They flow. Sometimes, the current is swift and forceful. Sometimes, the emotions are like a waterfall, a tsunami, a whirlpool. Other times, feelings are seemingly frozen in place, like a glacier. And often, surprisingly, even in grief, the feelings can be tranquil, like a still lake.

Today

What form of water best reflects your grief today?

August 3

Transcendence is about being above, being able to see from a new perspective. Transcending loss means viewing loss as a larger whole, and in doing so, making meaning from your loss. Although seeing from a greater vantage point generally comes only with time, you can know that it is possible.

Today

Be open to transcendence.

August 4

Gratitude is a spiritual practice. Certainly, when grieving, it's easy to focus on all that is lost and all that is wrong in the world. Challenge yourself today to focus on something you're grateful for in your life: your friends who support you, your surviving loved ones, the sunshine, your home, your faith, your health, and the love that still, now and forever, permeates your life.

Today

Breathe in gratitude. Breathe out resentment.

August 5

You are not alone. If you cry in the night, others are doing the same. If you wonder how you'll move forward, others feel confused, too. If you miss your loved one with every fiber of your being, you are surrounded by others who feel likewise. You are part of a network of grieving people everywhere. Fortunately, love is stronger than, bigger than, and more powerful than grief.

Today

Remember that you are not alone.

August 6

If you shut yourself off from experiencing pain, you also shut yourself off from experiencing joy. In other words, when you truncate your feelings, you suppress them across the board. You may think that you're protecting yourself, but actually you are dooming yourself to a half-lived life.

Today

Take the risk to feel pain so that you might feel joy again one day.

August 7

Examine your broken heart and look deeply into its cracks. In the midst of the brokenness, can you find a richer sense of compassion? A deeper understanding of love? A more empathic understanding of suffering? A broader sense of unconditional love? Your heart may be broken, but it doesn't have to become bitter. Look at the cracks, and notice how they let light stream in.

Today

Let light shine into your brokenness.

August 8

Although sometimes words will provide comfort, the truth is that no words can ultimately take pain away. Sometimes, the power of touch can succeed where words fail. It could be a hug, a hand held, or a cheek caressed. If you don't have someone near you who can offer a loving touch, then hug yourself, a pet, or a favorite stuffed animal.

Today

Use touch to offer comfort to yourself.

August 9

It is shocking over and over again when you realize that your loved one really isn't going to walk through the door anymore. It feels like a kick in the gut when the realization sinks in deeply, again and again. Their form on this planet is gone. There is a terrible sadness in finally "getting it," that they are not coming back through the door.

Today

Notice how your realization of your loss has shifted over time.

August 10

You are stronger than you know. When you get out of
bed though it would be easier to stay in it; when you let
yourself cry; when you courageously face your pain; when
you keep functioning and paying the bills and feeding the
children . . . Notice how strong you are, even when you
feel weak.

Today

Know that you have a core strength that allows you to
keep on living even when it is a struggle.

August 11

The physical experience of grief can be especially intense.
Sometimes, there is an ache, a pain in the heart that is
mirrored by pain in the body. You may feel tightness in
the chest, a knot in your belly, a sharpness that doubles
you over. Over time, the physical symptoms should start
to lessen in intensity . . . or at least occur less frequently.

Today

Be gentle with your body.

August 12

Life is constantly flowing. When you resist the current
of "what is," you create even more suffering for yourself. Life for you has flowed in a direction that you don't
want. However, to the degree that you resist and deny it,
you will suffer more. Swimming against the current is
exhausting and futile. If you will sink into the current,
open to it, flow with it, and learn from it with curiosity,
you will suffer less.

Today

Drop your resistance. Let yourself be carried by the flow
of your pain, by your grief, by the way of things.

August 13

Grief is like a winding road. You go forward, you go
backward, you loop around, you backtrack, you round a
corner . . . Do not judge yourself on this unpredictable
journey. Grief will take you to places that you never
imagined, that you didn't even know existed.

Today

Be patient with yourself and with the extremely nonlin-
ear process of grieving.

August 14

Each of us holds many roles in our lifetime: daughter/son, wife/husband, sister/brother, mother/father, employee/entrepreneur, athlete/singer, *griever*. But if you look under these and other powerful and important roles, you'll find that you are more than the roles. You are a deep and vast, spacious essence . . . a soul that moves in wisdom.

Today

Close your eyes and feel the spacious stillness within you.

August 15

Do not seek closure. It isn't desirable, nor is it even possible. Seek instead integration. You are on a journey of integrating loss into your life, learning to live with heartbreak, learning to hold eternal love in your heart. The bridge back to life means you will synthesize loss and love in your life, simultaneously.

Today

Since closure doesn't exist, start to think about synthesis as your goal.

August 16

Like a turtle, there will be times when you come out of
your shell (of grief), and there will be other times when
you simply cannot come out. On those days when you
need to draw in, let yourself hunker down and stay in
your shell. Give yourself permission to hide away. Don't
judge your feelings or force them to change.

Today

Simply be where you need to be and allow yourself the
space you need.

August 17

Perhaps your loved one did something hurtful to you
when you were alive. Perhaps you never reconciled with
them. It's time to forgive them for being human. Forgiveness does not mean that you condone what they did. It
simply means that you cut your attachment to anger and
resentment. Forgiveness is for your own peace of mind.

Today

Put down your grudge. Let yourself be at peace.

August 18

Some days you have glimmers of peace, a smile, maybe even a laugh. And sometimes you feel guilty for having these glimpses of pure beauty. Put the guilt down. Know that when you are able to savor life, even with a tinge of sorrow, you honor your dear one's life and their love. Playing small doesn't honor them. Living with an open heart does.

Today

Let glimmers of sunshine in and know that as you keep living, you honor your loved one.

August 19

Love is a gift. It makes you feel richer, deeper, and brighter. When a loved one is gone, it feels like the gift is gone, too. But actually, the essence of the gift remains. Remember that you are a different person because of their love. Although you long for them, the gift—their love—remains with you now and forever.

Today

Let yourself feel the extraordinary grace of the gift of love in your life.

August 20

It is common for people to try to minimize your pain: "Oh but you had so many years together." "You're young, you'll have other children." "You'll find someone else." "It was only a pet." People do this because they have such a hard time tolerating pain (yours or theirs). Know that your pain is acceptable. You don't need to minimize it or anyone else's.

Today

Recognize that your pain is real and necessary.

August 21

Resilience has to do with the ability to bounce back or cope with adversity. Of course, as grief stretches you, you acquire a new shape. You stretch; you retract; you pull; you knot inward, you stretch again. It is our nature to be adaptive and resilient. You have that capacity within you.

Today

Think about how grief is stretching you.

August 22

People will say that time heals all wounds. It doesn't, not alone. You must also allow yourself to grieve, to ride the cycles of pain, to share with others, to reach out, to draw in, to turn toward grief, to express your feelings, to learn, and then (bit by bit) begin to embrace life. Then time will be on your side.

Today

Let time work for you.

August 23

It can be easy to fall into the trap of bitterness, raging against "what is." Perhaps you're feeling victimized, punished, disgusted by life. It's understandable that you would feel this way, but remember that there is another way—a way that awakens you to something more. On the path to transcendence, you acknowledge the sorrow of your reality; but you also look for a different way to be with it. You accept and you open.

Today

Breathe in the feeling of awakening. Breathe out the feeling of bitterness.

August 24

With grief, there can be such an ache in your heart that you feel you can't breathe. You are almost thrown to the ground with such heavy heartache. Know that these pangs are a natural part of the journey.

Today

The intensity of your grief will space itself out, shifting and changing over time.

August 25

Grieving is an exhausting process. Your emotional, spiritual, and physical energy is zapped by so much sorrow and mixed emotions. You must let yourself rest. Give yourself permission to let things go, say no when you can. Restrict your activities so that you can rest as much as possible.

Today

Let yourself say no today.

August 26

One of the most common places to cry is in the car, while you are driving. Something about being alone and having a moment to feel seems to loosen the tears. Let them flow (as long as you can safely drive . . . otherwise, pull over). Wherever you feel comfortable, let it be your safe place for tears. Don't apologize, don't judge—tears are nature's way of flushing emotions through the body.

Today

Be open to the moment when tears flow. They are an expression of the tender heart.

August 27

Some people find that after a major loss, they feel a more intense connection to a higher power. They may find comfort in a sense of spiritual presence. However, other people find that they lose their faith completely—and may even have overwhelming anger toward God. Either way, you have permission to be where you are and feel what you feel.

Today

Believer, atheist, or agnostic—trust your process.

August 28

Your loved ones are like stars in the heaven . . . They shine upon you and watch over you. Did you know that when a star dies, its light continues to shine through the universe for billions of years? Your loved ones' light continues to shine on you and out from within you.

Today

Hold your loved ones' light close to your heart.

August 29

So much of loss is about change and transformation. Your loved one has transformed into a new form, one that is unseen but still vibrant. And you too are transforming into a new you, one breath at a time. Ask your loved one to assist you as you adapt to these dramatic transformations. Although you may feel stuck in your cocoon, remember that time is required for the butterfly to emerge.

Today

Be open to seen and unseen transformation. Be open to a time when your wings will spread.

August 30

When you are feeling sorrow, think of something that your loved one did that made you smile. Take a few minutes and enjoy the memory, expand the thought to a feeling . . . a feeling of love and lightness. Think how enriched you are because of such a memory, such an experience. Think how diminished you would be if you had never had that experience, and thus didn't have this memory in your heart.

Today

Know that you hold each beloved memory, each smile, within you even as you grieve.

August 31

When the physical form of your dear one is gone, it
is tempting to believe that they are completely gone.
Instead, know that their body was only their shell. Their
spirit is with you and beyond you. I believe that each of
us will reunite with the spirit of our loved ones when the
time is right. Although you long to see their shell again,
long to touch and hold it, remember that their essence,
their most vital core self, is with you now and always.

Today

How do you feel if you believe that you will be reunited
again, in spirit, with your beloved? Hold on to that
feeling.

September 1

There will be days when you feel like you're going crazy. You may find that you lose things, are forgetful, and can't concentrate. Grieving takes up so much psychic energy that there isn't much focus left for the details of getting through life. However, you won't always feel this scattered. Over time, you'll have more minor episodes, and they'll happen less frequently. Be patient and tender with yourself. Cut yourself some slack as you get through one day at a time.

Today

Although you may feel at times that you're going nuts, rest assured that you are not. You are simply experiencing the crazy journey of grieving.

September 2

It's not unusual for grievers to experience signs from their beloved in the guise of nature. It could be an unusual cloud display, or a lingering bird, butterfly, or wild animal. Sometimes, people look for otherworldly signs (and those happen as well), but the sign you experience might be as simple as a rainbow or a birdcall. Look to nature . . . Listen for simple signs.

Today

Know that your loved one is closer than you think.

September 3

It's easy to feel like there is no longer any future. The anticipated and planned future in your imagination has been wiped away. Rather than look ahead with dread, fear, or bewilderment, keep your attention firmly on this moment. This moment is all you actually have. Be in the now, and you will gradually live your way into that future.

Today

Keep your focus on one moment at a time.

September 4

Grief is easier to bear if you believe that you'll be reunited with your loved one when the time is right. Those who believe this still suffer, but they suffer less. Since no one can prove it (or not) absolutely, why not be open to the possibility? Why not hold out that hope?

Today

What would it feel like if you suspended doubt and simply believed?

September 5

There will be times when you wonder, *How will I ever survive this?* You may even ask this daily. The answer is that you will survive this because you have a core of resilient strength within you. While you may not be in touch with it, it is there, deep inside. With time and intention, you can connect to this strength and it will help sustain you.

Today

Reflect on the core of you. Allow yourself to notice aspects of your inner strength.

September 6

Who are you becoming? Grief changes you, and it's easy to see how it might only change you for the worse (if you let yourself become more sad, more bitter, more fearful). Can you allow grief to make you softer, wiser, more compassionate? How would your loved one want you to change?

Today

Think about intentionally changing in a way that would make your loved one proud of you.

September 7

There are so many kinds of loss that we encounter throughout our lives—changing jobs and careers, moving out of homes, illness, divorce, children growing up, estrangement, loss of loved ones, loss of beloved pets, loss of our youth, loss of our innocence. This is part of the human condition and part of the price tag of living. Never forget that love endures, enriches, and follows you from one chapter to the next in the book of your life.

Today

Are life and love worth the price tag of loss?

September 8

Because you are still alive, there is a reason for you to be here. You may not know what that purpose is yet—it may take awhile to discern—but it's no accident that you are here. Perhaps your soul has more growing to do, or you have something to give to another. Perhaps you will discover a new purpose for your days. Take time to be still, quiet, and present to your intuition.

Today

Ask your loved one for guidance and be open to the answer.

September 9

Most people are absolutely terrified of death. As a griever, however, your relationship to death may have completely changed. There may be no more fear. In fact, you may look forward to the time when you will leave your earthly body . . . a joyous reunion of souls is sure to take place.

Today

Notice if you regard your own death with a new perspective.

September 10

Every day with a loved one matters. We cannot assume that we will have a tomorrow together. In fact, you know better than anyone that life is uncertain. Let grief teach you to embrace the living *now*, and to live in a way in which you will have no regrets.

Today

Remember life, not just death.

September 11

Does holding on to pain keep you closer to your loved one? Some people are afraid to begin to let their pain dissipate because they believe they will lose their loved one all over again. You will always have some pain in your heart, but as time passes you will still stay deeply connected through love.

Today

You don't need pain to remain close to your dear one.

September 12

If there are things you wish you could have said . . . perhaps the words "I'm sorry" or words of good-bye . . . write them down. Write them in a journal or letter to your loved one and pour your heart out. It's possible to take care of unfinished business even if the other person is not here physically. Writing engages a therapeutic process.

Today

Write to your loved one. Let them know if you have any regrets or any unspoken words.

September 13

Listen inside to what it is you need to do for your grief today. Do you need to cry, to write, to be silent? Do you need to help someone, reach out, volunteer? Do you need to set up a memorial or wrap yourself in a blanket? You have permission to do what feels right for you today. Your journey is unique to you.

Today

Listen inside for your own true guidance to healing.

September 14

Self-compassion: For some this is simple; for others, it is a major challenge. Taking care of you and being gentle with yourself is so important. Try seeing yourself as you were when you were a child . . . an innocent, tender being. See if you can summon compassion for that little girl or boy, and lavish your kindness upon her or him.

Today

Put your hand over your heart and breathe in tenderness.

September 15

Birthdays and anniversaries, holidays and angelversaries—they can be so full of sorrow and pain. Sometimes, the anticipation of the day is even worse than the day itself. Remember that these days are heavy with grief *and* potentially light with love at the same time. Focus on the love that will be with you forever. Focus on the fact that you even had this person in your life at all. Focus on the fact that nothing can take that love out of your soul, not now and not ever.

Today

How will you honor the next big day?

September 16

Transcendence is a choice. If you use the SOAR acronym
to guide you, you can notice the ways in which you transcend loss: Spirituality, Outreach, Attitude, and Rein-
vestment. Which pathway to meaning calls you? Are you
drawn to grow and change in one or more of these ways?
See if you can awaken your desire to *insist* that your loved
one's death has a meaningful outcome.

Today

If you can't choose transcendence today, perhaps you will
be able to tomorrow.

September 17

Sea glass: rough, sharp edges worn down by time and salt and tumbling. Like broken glass, the jagged edges of your grief will be softened by time as well . . . that is, if you let yourself grieve. (Otherwise, time will simply pass, and your grief will remain sharp and buried, waiting for you to tend to it.) The beauty of sea glass is like the beauty of love that remains in your heart forever.

Today

The rough edges of your grief will eventually be worn into something softer.

September 18

Many people believe that grief is a process that is completed within a few weeks or months. In reality, grief is a lifelong process that will change and evolve over time. As with any process, it must unfold. You cannot know anything but how you feel today. The future will be evident once it arrives. Be patient with the journey, and watch as it moves forward, cycles back, takes you deeper, lifts you higher, and cycles back again.

Today

Be aware that resisting the natural process of grief only increases your suffering.

September 19

Some people cannot summon tears of grief. Numbness prevents any tears from shedding. If this is your experience, let it be. You cannot force tears if they do not wish to fall. All you can do is stay present to your experience and observe. Tears are not required in order to feel.

Today

Do not judge yourself if tears do not come.

September 20

Keep photographs of your loved ones nearby. Do not listen to others who might tell you to take them down or hide them away. While photos may exacerbate your pain at first, a shift will occur with time so that they bring a smile to your face. Photos are a gentle reminder of immense love.

Today

Blow a kiss to your photographs of loved ones.

September 21

It is the nature of grief to come in microbursts, even many years after the loss. Do not be surprised by these storm clouds of emotion. Just let them blow through you. Have compassion for yourself, and watch the tempest arise and pass away.

Today

Remember that just as love is a part of your life, grief is as well.

September 22

They say that pets who have died go to the rainbow bridge and wait for their beloved people-parents to join them. It is important to acknowledge that pet loss can be profound and deep. Often people minimize this loss, saying that they were "only" a dog, a cat, a horse, a bunny. Yet, we frequently develop intense unconditional love relationships with animals. In fact, these dear relationships can be unusually pure and uncomplicated, with no drama or conflict.

Today

Know that the loss of a beloved pet deserves to be honored with love.

September 23

In a world that knows sorrow, pain, tragedy, and horror, try to focus on one thing today that is beautiful. Take a moment and notice a pure, simple blessing: a flower, a shadow, a shell, a smile, the face of your loved one in a photograph. Drink in a moment of grace in spite of sadness.

Today

Give gratitude for one single instance of beauty.

September 24

Do not be surprised if sometimes beloved memories slice like a knife. They can feel utterly devastating as the yearning, the palpable longing, floods your heart. Know that these painful memories highlight loss, yes, but they also highlight the blessing of love in your life.

Today

Memories are double-edged: they highlight love and loss simultaneously.

September 25

You can grieve with resistance or you can grieve with acceptance. Grieving with resistance uses extra energy that exhausts you and wears you down. Grieving with a nonjudgmental acceptance, a willingness to be with what is, allows you to bend with the wind rather than push against it.

Today

Align yourself with the pace of grief in your life.

September 26

Living with loss means that you must ride the waves of grief. Some waves will knock you to your knees; other waves will be gentle. They come and they go. Surf the waves, riding each one's natural cycle. And when you can, let yourself float until the next wave arises.

Today

Be aware that although waves will continue, eventually they will come less frequently.

September 27

You are part of a vast web of people around the world: people who long, who grieve, who get up each morning with heartache, who hurt, who keep loving, who are filled with eternal unceasing love. You are connected to all humanity.

Today

Know that you are a strand in the web, a part of the whole.

September 28

Why? Why did this happen? Why is he gone? The question "Why?" is an expression of deep pain. The truth is that we simply cannot know why—we are too limited in our understanding. We don't know why some people live short lives and others live long ones. And even if we did know why, it wouldn't bring back our loved one. "Why?" is an expression of pain.

Today

Understand that "Why?" doesn't really have an answer.

September 29

Your loved one is beside you in spirit, next to you in your heart, and with you in memory. They are a part of who you were then, are now, and will be in the future. You are who you are because you continue to love them. You are *you* because their life and their death make an impact on you.

Today

Breathe in the blessing of their love.

September 30

Can you imagine how your loved one would have grieved if you had died first? Would they be able to function, to live with loss, to tolerate the pain? Is it possible that you have spared them that suffering? Can you think of bearing the pain now so they don't have to?

Today

Imagine yourself sparing your loved one from the burden of grieving you.

October 1

Lighting a candle can be a beautiful, symbolic way of keeping your loved one's ever-blessed presence around you. As you watch the flame flicker, think of their light still shining upon you and out from within you. Blowing out the candle can be symbolic as well, releasing their soul to the next place, knowing that you are always connected and eternally together.

Today

Light a candle in honor of your dear one.

October 2

You may have a lot of support right after your loss, usually up to a month after the funeral. But gradually, folks go back to their lives and you're left holding your grief on your own. Reach out for support from people who understand. It can be jarring to realize that others can move on but you have been changed forever.

Today

Be gentle with yourself.

October 3

You can use the power of visualization to summon an image of your dear one. How often do you take the time to actually bring to mind the delicate details of your loved one's face? Imagine yourself in a beautiful place (a meadow, by a lake) and visualize seeing your dear one. Imagine hugging your dear one. Imagine putting your hand on their face. Know that they are with you and within you, always.

Today

Close your eyes and call to mind the details of your dear one's face.

October 4

When you are in the dark valley of grieving, it seems impossible that light will ever come again. You see nothing but darkness in all directions. But the miracle is that light does come . . . it comes in the return of color, in memories that comfort, in love that lives on, in compassion and meaning and service to others.

Today

Look for the tiny shafts of light that peek through your dark grief.

October 5

Grief is the most arduous, exhausting, gut-wrenching, heartbreaking emotional work that you will most likely ever do. It takes so much energy. Know that you are strong as you cry, as you wail, as you collapse from the weight of the sorrow. Know you are strong as you face your feelings and hold on to the love that whispers through your soul.

Today

Although you may not feel brave, you are courageous in your brokenness.

October 6

You may be thinking that life isn't fair . . . and it isn't. It's not fair that people die before living a full life cycle. It's not fair that some people have an abundance of resources while others have so few. No, life isn't about fairness. Life is about love. You can know that love has graced your life.

Today

Focus on the blessings of love in your life and not merely on the injustices of life.

October 7

The landscape of loss changes through the years. In fact, the landscape can change from day to day and even moment to moment. Desert, mountain, forest, jungle, lake . . . it can be a draining journey. The landscape will change every day. What won't change, however, is the love for your dear one—that love is embedded within you and will be your constant companion no matter what terrain you find yourself.

Today

Navigate whatever landscape arises.

October 8

How are you treating grief? Do you see grief as an enemy, an unwelcome intruder, a monster? What would happen if you softened your stance . . . if you viewed grief as a teacher, a guide? What would happen if you asked to see its wisdom and then listened? What might you hear?

Today

Sit and listen to what grief has to tell you.

October 9

Just as a rose is still beautiful even when it has many thorns, life is still beautiful even with the thorn of painful loss. As you feel the sharp pain of grief, keep your eye on the love that rests within you. Focus on the beauty of the rose.

Today

Remember that love and loss are inextricably joined.

October 10

The goal in life is not to avoid pain. If that were the case, you should never open your heart—and what a sad life that would be. The goal is to love and to grow—grief offers the opportunity for both.

Today

Recognize that you have not avoided pain. In fact, you have loved deeply.

October 11

It's easy to think of your loved one as a saint, as if they had no irritating characteristics. You have permission to remember them as a full human being with strengths *and* weaknesses. You are allowed to recall the hard times as well as the good, the struggles as well as the joys. In fact, it honors them to remember the truth of who they were and who you were together. Love is big enough to encompass all of it.

Today

Remember that no one is perfect and love embraces all truths.

October 12

Do you ever worry that you're doing grief wrong? Some days you are feeling better, and then, as if you've turned a corner, *wham*! Something sends you reeling back into grief. Guess what? That's part of the process. Like an arrow in a bow, you have to go backward before you can shoot forward. Trust your own unique process for healing.

Today

There isn't a wrong way to do grief. There is only your way.

October 13

So often we want to shut down in our grief, close off to life, love, and vulnerability. Is that what your loved one would want for you? As time continues to pass, ask yourself how you can open to the call of life. Can you live with more compassion, more depth, more love, less fear?

Today

Although you may not feel like opening to life just yet, continue to hold out the possibility.

October 14

You are blessed. You were blessed to have your loved one in your life, and you're still blessed because they are now and forever part of you. Just because their form is gone doesn't mean the gift of their love is gone. Their love is woven into you. Their influence is part of your daily experience. Your loved ones will ease your way when it is your time to cross over.

Today

Though it may be hard to feel this, remember that you are blessed.

October 15

No matter how BIG your grief feels (and it often feels huge), you are bigger than your grief. Your soul is more expansive, deeper, and vaster than the pain that colors your perspective right now. Even when you don't feel it, know that inner spaciousness is part of you.

Today

Close your eyes and imagine a core within you, like the core of an apple. See if you can connect to the quiet and still strength at your core.

October 16

The paradox of pain is that if you try to resist and avoid it, your suffering actually increases. It may *seem* that your suffering increases when you feel it fully. But, in truth, going into the heart of pain—deep into the valley of it—is what moves you forward and eventually leads to healing. That is the purpose of feeling your pain.

Today

Look at your pain. Observe its shape, color, texture. Notice, and watch it shift.

October 17

If your loved ones were looking down on you, watching you in your sorrow, what would they say about your grieving process? What advice might they send your way? Do you think they would be proud of how you are managing? Would they be heartbroken that you are in such agony? Would they understand?

Today

Imagine what your loved ones would tell you about grief.

October 18

The root of the word *bereavement* cuts to the heart of grief. It means "to rob." Grief can feel like that—being robbed of something precious. And of course, being robbed, you might feel extremely angry. However, remember that while you are robbed of your loved one's physical form, their love and spirit are never taken from you.

Today

Love transcends death because love is emotion and energy, without form.

October 19

Grief is a roller coaster. One day you feel a bit better, a bit more energetic, and then *wham!* you're rocketing into that abyss of darkness. This can happen hour to hour, day to day, week to week. Don't try to resist the ride . . . be patient with yourself and know that the ups and downs will continue to come even as they eventually space apart more evenly.

Today

Be aware that you are not alone on this roller coaster.

October 20

Many people find that nighttime is the hardest time of day. The dark of night is when the world quiets and you find yourself alone with your grief. Instead of dreading this time, try seeing it as a chance to connect with your loved one—and an opportunity to feel your feelings.

Today

See what gifts the night can bring to you as you mourn.

October 21

When it begins to feel like it's time to shift your energies and move forward, remember that your loved one is always beside you. When you move forward, you never leave them behind. You can let go of any guilt because you deserve to keep living . . . just know that they are right beside you, cheering you on.

Today

Never forget that your loved one is an inextricable part of who you are.

October 22

Simple comforts can be a big help when you're grieving:
Notice and intentionally invite comfort into your life—
perhaps taking a walk in the woods, playing with a pet, lighting a candle, watching a funny movie, talking to a friend,
hugging a loved one, taking a hot bath, curling up with a
warm blanket, listening to music, reading poetry, wood-
working, fishing, enjoying some fresh cookies and milk.

Today

Sprinkle your day with moments of pure self-care.

October 23

A secondary loss means losing your loved one *and* something else: losing a role (as a wife or mother), losing a
place in the community (like at a school or business),
losing friends, losing the person who made the Thanksgiving turkey, losing your faith, losing your place in the
world of couples, etc. Secondary losses are multilayered,
real, and very painful.

Today

Acknowledge that you have lost more than just a dear
loved one.

October 24

Most people don't understand the magnitude of loss or its life-changing process. Because of your experience, you are now something of a grief ambassador. You can educate others bit by bit with a gentle explanation that it's good to feel, it's vital to remember, it's essential to talk about our loved ones, and it's a fact that life has changed irrevocably.

Today

Explain to someone else what you know about the life-long impact of grief.

October 25

Imagine for a moment a world in which your loved one had never even existed. Imagine what your life would have been like. Imagine how different you would have been. When you feel yourself getting overwhelmed by the tidal wave of grief, try shifting your attention to how your life unfolded because of your dear one.

Today

Reflect on how your soul was touched by your loved one, and remember all the abundance you received that remains a part of you today.

October 26

Look at your heart. Is it open and full of the love that you continue to share with your loved one? Or is it shut down, closed by grief and pain? If you're feeling stuck in bitterness or sorrow, try creating flow in your life. Emotions need to flow . . . energy needs to flow. Try reaching out to someone today with no other purpose than to assist them, and see if your heart subtly shifts.

Today

Remember that hearts are happiest when they are open.

October 27

Look up into the heavens and gaze at the stars. When you see a light shining, it's quite possible that that particular star is no longer alive. In fact, when a star dies, its light continues to shine for billions of years. So does the light of your loved one.

Today

Let your loved one shine upon you and out from within you.

October 28

Staying in touch with your dear loved one through writing is a way to nurture the continuing bond between you. You can write a letter and send it to the sky with a balloon. You can release a letter in a river or lake. You can journal to your loved one. Keep your connection vibrant.

Today

Death has not ended your relationship.

October 29

Are you getting too attached to your label as griever? Bereaved parent, widow/widower, orphan, or victim, it can be easy to cling to this label as a way of identifying your experience. However, you are more than this label. Try expanding your identification to include survivor, thriver, someone who triumphs over adversity, believer, leader by example. Add some new labels to who you are, and see what shifts.

Today

What identity would you like to be living into?

October 30

In the old days, grievers were not encouraged to talk about their loved ones. Now we recognize how important it is to talk about dear ones, to share stories, to remember. Learning to live with loss is about staying connected to your loved one even as you embrace the living. Be the one who talks about the elephant in the room.

Today

Share a story with a friend, a family member, or even a stranger.

October 31

Holidays bring up lots of feelings, and Halloween can be especially painful for bereaved parents of children who would have been trick-or-treating. It seems so unfair that other children gather their treats while your child does not. Life wasn't supposed to unfold in this manner. Sometimes, the pain seems unbearable . . . just breathe into that pain, letting it rise within you and shift.

Today

Know that you never have to let go of love.

November 1

One step at a time. That's all you can do. Just this hour and then the next. Looking too far ahead can flood you with anxiety and fear. All you have is this particular moment on this particular day. Let grief teach you about the importance of being in the now.

Today

Breathe in this moment to the count of five. Hold your breath for the count of five. Exhale to the count of five. Be in this moment.

November 2

Grief is an invisible wound. It's not obvious that you are hurting, devastated, crushed. In the Victorian era, grievers wore a black armband to signify to the world that they were in mourning. The message was, "Handle with care; I am grieving." But today, you must forge ahead without a warning label.

Today

You know that you are wounded. Handle yourself with care.

November 3

Your memories are like a bright light within your grief. Although the memories may also feel painful, as they highlight the loss, just imagine if you had no memories. Imagine if you had never known them or couldn't remember knowing them.

Today

Hold your memories in your heart and cherish them, for they are evidence of a great life that intersected with your own.

November 4

What if you knew that your loved one was watching over you? What if you were certain that his or her presence was with you all the time and that your love was unshakeable, stronger than death?

Today

Be open to sensing, intuiting, and being with the profound unbreakable bond of love beyond form.

November 5

When you allow yourself to feel deep pain, to go down into the valley of the shadow, you also open yourself to eventually feeling deep joy. In other words, your pain has a purpose. The opposite, shutting down your emotional life, keeps your grief hidden. However, even as you protect yourself from feeling pain, you also stop yourself from feeling joy. The purpose of feeling your entire emotional range is that it is part of the richness of being alive.

Today

Let yourself feel the depth of your despair, knowing that it will open you to great joy as well.

November 6

There is a difference between acute grief and subtle grief. Acute grief can last a few weeks to a few years. During this time, grief seems to take up the foreground of your life. As the years pass, however, as you process and express your feelings, grief moves to being the subtle background of your life. Grief becomes a thread in your life, but not the entire tapestry. Trust this process to unfold.

Today

Are you experiencing acute or subtle grief?

November 7

Think of grief like a spiral: You seem to be going around in circles, but actually you are coming around to a new level. Sometimes you go deeper and sometimes you transcend higher. Both ends of the spiral are real and true.

Today

Trust your spiraling process, and remember that your loved one is beside you on your journey.

November 8

Although human hearts break, they also heal. The spirit is ultimately resilient, resourceful, and transcendent. Do not rush your grief. Lean into its sharpness, and know that feeling deeply leads to deep healing.

Today

Believe that you are a resilient soul.

November 9

You might hear the expression from well-meaning friends, "It's time to move on." What does that really mean? It means moving forward *with* your loved one ever in your heart, a breath away. It means choosing to reengage with life. It means relating with others even as you stay connected to your beloved, who is closer than you think.

Today

Know that you can move forward with your loved one in your heart. There are opportunities and blessings that life still has to offer.

November 10

Anticipation of an event is sometimes harder than the actual event. So if you are having trouble anticipating the holidays ahead, know that it is quite normal to feel like you are falling apart as the season approaches. Often the day itself is not as bad as the pre-season dread. In fact, the day itself is an occasion to celebrate love and be grateful for your loved ones' continuing impact on your life.

Today

See the holiday preparations as part of the process, and breathe into them.

November 11

Be cautious of the word (and concept) of "closure." Although we may long for closure, it's actually a myth. You cannot close the door on your feelings and seal them away. And you certainly wouldn't want to close the door on your loved one. Instead, look forward to a degree of healing while embracing the fact that you are always connected in obvious and mysterious ways.

Today

Let go of the fantasy of closure.

November 12

A grieving mother consulted a wise, holy man about how to bring her son back to life. The holy man told her to bring him a mustard seed from a house that had never known sorrow. She began her quest to find such a home. However, wherever she went, she found others who knew death. She stayed and listened to their stories. There were others who grieved deeply, whose hearts were broken, who cried into their pillows at night. In time, her heavy heart lifted as she offered compassion to those who suffered as she had.

Today

Know that you are not alone.

November 13

How do you find expression for your feelings? There are
a variety of ways to express your anger, your sadness, your
confusion, your despair: sing, write poetry, build something, create a contemplative collage, sculpt with Play-
Doh, doodle, or paint colors and shapes that express your
grief. There is relief in getting that which is within you
out of you.

Today

Do not judge the product of your efforts. All expressive
energy is part of the process.

November 14

Your dear one's life affected others. Your dear one's death
affected others. How you grieve and grow affects others.
The ripple effect of a single life is enormous. Be sure to
share stories, share the impact, share the love so that the
ripples continue to widen.

Today

Notice how all things are connected, one being affecting
another.

November 15

Some people feel that their grief connects them to their loved one. If they let it fade, they will lose their sense of connection. It's important to note that your pain isn't what keeps you tethered to your loved one. You are bound together through love. You can stay connected by blowing a morning kiss to a photograph, talking to them while you drive in the car, visiting the cemetery, writing them notes, listening to your heart . . . whatever feels right to you.

Today

Pain isn't required for an ongoing connection with your loved one.

November 16

So many people get worked up about the small stuff—traffic jams, deadlines, dusty shelves, being late, even overcooked food. After losing a loved one, you gain a different perspective on life. The little things begin to matter very little. They all feel insignificant in the context of life and death, in the face of the precious moments we have with our loved ones.

Today

Use your broader perspective to stop sweating the small stuff.

November 17

When the ache, the longing, the yearning overwhelms you, let yourself lean into it. Acknowledge your feelings as a true response. And then, pair those hard feelings with a breath of gratitude: Remember a beautiful memory that lives in you and makes you who you are. When you honor the pain and overlay it with awareness of the gift of love, you lighten the heaviness of grief.

Today

Both grief and love are true simultaneously. Hold them both in your heart.

November 18

Grief changes you. If you expect to go back to being
the same person you were before your loss, you will be
disappointed. That person is gone. It might be tempting
to look at all the unwanted ways you've changed (being
fearful or sad, feeling diminished). Instead, look at the
healthy ways you've changed, how you are becoming wiser,
stronger, more compassionate, more understanding, and
more expansive.

Today

Let your loss add layers of complexity to who you are.

November 19

The Latin root of *suffer* means "to bear." In our Western
culture, we typically have trouble bearing pain, allowing
it to be. Thus, it takes courage to bear it and experience
it. By experiencing it fully, you allow it to shift and transform. Know that in allowing the suffering of grief, it will
begin to move through you and become more bearable.

Today

Watch your grief as a compassionate witness. Let it be.

November 20

Separation is an illusion. Though your loved one is not physically with you, they are with you spiritually and energetically. They live in you and through you. They are ever with you, as close as your breath. When you are overwhelmed with missing their form, remember that their essence is woven into the fabric of you, now and forever.

Today

You are less apart than you may imagine.

November 21

For Thanksgiving, whenever it falls this year, you may not be feeling grateful for your grief, but you are grateful that you had your loved one in your life. And they continue to be part of your life in a new way. So focus on your gratitude for their birth, for their life, for their love for you, and for your enrichment through loving them. Keep your focus on that gratitude, and the mountain of this holiday won't be quite as treacherous.

Today

Light a candle or put a plate under your plate to symbolize the presence of your dear one.

November 22

Some days you will have glimmers of sunlight with your grief, some days scattered showers, and other days torrential storms. Just as all kinds of weather are necessary for living things to grow, all expressions of grief are necessary for your own personal growth. If you have heavy storms today, do not resist. Surrender to the rain.

Today

Remember that the weather is always changing.

November 23

Self-compassion is so important but is often extremely difficult. You might feel so overcome by your feelings that you forget to be kind to yourself. You are a dear, broken-hearted soul who needs the soft touch of loving-kindness toward yourself.

Today

Put your hand on your heart and summon the love you feel for your loved one. Feel that dear, tender love, and then turn it toward yourself, absorbing it into your heart.

November 24

Is stoicism strength? Sometimes, grievers get complimented for being "strong" when they function well and show no signs of "falling apart." However, it's the falling apart that takes the most fearlessness. Give yourself permission to cry, to hurt, to feel, to come unglued . . . therein lies your courage, your healing, and your growth.

Today

Do not confuse having a stiff upper lip with strength.

November 25

Do you like to visit the cemetery? Is it comforting for you to visit where ashes have been scattered? It's certainly healthy to visit a place where you can put flowers, stones, and trinkets in honor of your dear one. However, if you prefer to stay away, that's okay, too. Trust your intuition about what you need for your grieving process. Whatever you choose, know that you can connect with your dear one wherever you go and wherever you are.

Today

Discover the places that most help you summon a sense of connection to your loved one.

November 26

Your loved one is a gift to you in your life. Just because the gift changed in ways that you didn't anticipate or desire does not, in any way, lessen the value of the gift. The gift is ever-present in your heart and in your life.

Today

Let your loved one live on within you.

November 27

Grief comes in waves . . . sometimes intense tidal waves and sometimes gentle swells. They come and they recede, high tide and low tide. Learning to live with loss means knowing that it's normal for the waves of grief to continue through the rest of your life.

Today

Surf the waves.

November 28

Time alone won't move you through your grief. Decades of darkness could go by if you stuff your feelings, avoid pain, close your heart, and hunker down in bitterness. If, however, you feel your feelings, accept the pain, and make the decision to grow with grief, the years will brighten as they pass.

Today

Face your feelings, and let time be on your side.

November 29

Notice how your thoughts impact your feelings. It's normal to have thoughts such as *Why did this happen? This shouldn't have happened,* or *I can't survive this.* But over time, see if you can shift your thoughts to *I will make this have meaning, I will live in honor of my loved one,* or *I know that they're with me and that one day we'll be reunited.* Your thoughts are extremely powerful, and they will, over time, create your ongoing emotional experience.

Today

Notice which thoughts get the most airtime in your head.

November 30

It is not uncommon to have some kind of communication from a loved one. It could be a visitation in a dream, or some inexplicable sign, sound, image, or occurrence. You might also see telltale signs in nature that alert you to their presence—a cardinal, a turkey, a butterfly, a rainbow. Sometimes, you wish for a sign but it doesn't seem to come. Be open and let yourself be receptive to mystery.

Today

If you receive a sign or a visitation, give thanks.

December 1

Grief is a sort of hibernation of the soul. Grief asks you to draw in, to rest, to be quiet, to reflect. Though you must also go about the business of work and living, give over to the hibernation energy when you can. Spend time in the space of quiet healing. You cannot force it to be spring when you are in winter. While parts of your soul will always know the eternal winter, other seasons will shine again. It is nature's way.

Today

Let yourself hibernate quietly in order to heal.

December 2

You have permission to cut yourself some slack this holiday season. If you don't want to go into stores, then shop online. If you don't want to bake cookies or send out cards, then don't. Do the absolute minimum, and get help when you need it. You have permission to take care of yourself. Grieving takes extreme energy, so be gentle to yourself.

Today

Only say yes when it feels comfortable.

December 3

In the beginning of grief, you want and need to tell your story over and over again. It's important for the mind to start to integrate this new reality. Repetition is key to healthy grieving. You may want to replay the details: Where were you when you found out that your loved one died? Were you with them? What happened next? And then? Reviewing the experience isn't just a neurotic loop. Reliving and repeating the sequence of events is part of your healing.

Today

Let yourself mentally and verbally replay your story until it becomes a part of you.

December 4

True love never dies. Love that is deep, pure, and boundless is an eternal gift that mirrors the Divine. Although the physical form changes, the essence of that gift never wavers, not even for an instant. Though you fervently wish for the form (a hug, a kiss), know that the most essential parts of love are woven into the fabric of your soul, now and forever.

Today

Let true love give you the strength that will sustain you in the days ahead.

December 5

Grief knocks the wind out of you, leaving you flattened. If the support of friends and online communities doesn't feel like enough, consider finding a counselor to talk with. It's possible that medication could be helpful to you. Or, it could also be that connecting with a compassionate professional can help you unravel the knot of your grief.

Today

Do not hesitate to find a counselor, as needed.

December 6

A life is stunning no matter how brief. Our loved one stayed here as long as they were supposed to stay. We cannot know why. Although we can spend a lot of energy resisting the truth, by doing so we will only increase our suffering. Greater peace is found in making certain that their memory continues to touch others in a positive way.

Today

Breathe in what already is and breathe out love.

December 7

Fear of dying is the top fear among humans—higher than fear of public speaking and fear of dentists. However, after losing a loved one, your entire relationship to death has changed. Many grievers have no fear of death and in fact look forward to it as being a reunion with their loved ones. Grief takes the fear and sting out of the prospect of death.

Today

Release the fear of death from your life.

December 8

Stop for a moment, close your eyes, and tune in to your loved one. What would they say to you about your grieving? Would they tell you you're doing well? What could they say that would help you? What might they tell you to do while you still have time on the planet?

Today

Listen to heavenly advice.

December 9

There will be times when the ache of not being able to hold or hug your dear one will feel virtually unbearable. You would give anything for just one more hug. Know that this is very normal. Although a teddy bear is a poor substitute, find something to hug (a pillow, a stuffed animal, a friend) and hug it. A hug can sometimes comfort in ways that words cannot.

Today

Get a hug from a friend, from an animal, from a teddy bear.

December 10

Grief is not a mountain that you climb, reach the top, and then climb back down again. You won't be returning to your starting place. The grief journey moves slowly around the mountain, gradually moving up to new heights. This journey brings you to a place different from where you started. From this higher perspective, life and death will never look quite the same.

Today

Keep putting one foot in front of the other as you scale the mountain of grief.

December 11

The loss you are experiencing right now may feel overwhelming. And this loss might also trigger one or more losses from your past (even from your childhood). If this is the case, an even larger reservoir of grief may flood you. Let this be an invitation to drain some of the grief by revisiting losses from the past. Let this be an opportunity to engage in more growth and healing.

Today

Remember, it's never too late to grieve a loss from the past.

December 12

If you're finding this time of year to be a challenge, you are in good company. The ordinary stressors (time pressures, financial crunch, winter sadness) are compounded by the sorrow of grief. You may feel completely out of sync with the rest of the world. This holiday will come and go, just as the others do. Find small moments of solace in a smile, a candle, a song, a decoration. You will get through this.

Today

Take a deep breath and focus on just one moment at a time.

December 13

You never need to apologize for your grief. You don't need to apologize if you're crying, or if you need to hold the tears in. You have permission to bow out of events, parties, and family gatherings. You can choose to experience grief the way that you need to, independent of well-meaning friends' opinions.

Today

Trust your own process and let it be your way—no apologies necessary.

December 14

In the month or two after a major loss, you might find that you receive a lot of support, sympathy, and assistance. But gradually, others move on with their lives and you are left to deal with your grief on your own. It can feel overwhelming when support seemingly disappears. Some friends will drift away completely, while others stay but simply don't understand your experience.

Today

Find friends in an online grief community who understand your ongoing journey.

December 15

Sometimes there is a moment, when you first wake up in the morning, and then it strikes you: *My loved one is gone from this planet.* The sharp reality hits you right in the gut, and you almost lose your breath as the sinking feeling descends. Combine that terrible moment with a memory of goodness, and then hold on to the preciousness of the love that is ever-present.

Today

Remember that love ultimately transcends loss.

December 16

Some people are forever bitter and shut down after a major loss. Others find their pain to be an eventual springboard for deep growth. Often, there is a fork in the path of grief that offers a choice to go in one direction or another. Many people find that they must face this very intentional, conscious choice daily.

Today

Which direction will you choose?

December 17

Have you ever had the experience of being able to comfort another griever in a way that you knew was really helpful? Your loss gives you the skills to reach other grievers in a way that touches, moves, and supports. Grief can make you an empathic counselor full of the ability to offer solace to others.

Today

Being compassionate to other suffering souls is one way you can use your pain in a positive way.

December 18

If you are missing the experience of buying a holiday present for your loved one, try something different. Buy a gift in *honor* of your dear one—something that they would have enjoyed—and donate it to a local charity in their name. Consider libraries, hospitals, homeless shelters, women's shelters, and daycares, as potential places to gratefully give a gift. Your loved one can continue to touch others through your act of generosity.

Today

Giving is one of the ways to make meaning out of loss, even when loss feels meaningless.

December 19

When you lose a loved one, it can feel as if a part of you died with them. You are not the same person anymore. You need to allow yourself to grieve the loss of that part of you that is no more. Perhaps you are less innocent, less naive, less trusting. Perhaps you no longer have the explicit role of parent, of child, of spouse, of sibling. Acknowledge what is lost within yourself.

Today

Know that when something ends, something else begins . . . You are growing into that something new.

December 20

It can be hard to imagine a future when your present seems to have stopped. Perhaps you cannot even imagine how life will unfold now that everything has changed. The future is a big unknown, and you may feel utterly lost. One day at a time, you will begin living your way into the future. You will take the love that is part of you and start to share it with others. You will look around you and see who still needs your attention.

Today

As best as you can, trust that your future will begin to unfold itself before you, day by day.

December 21

Grieving is difficult work—it pulls the rug out from under your life. Many days feel intolerably dark, heavy, and agonizing. Know that on the stormiest of days, the sun shines above the clouds even when you cannot see it. There is still beautiful light in the world, and one day, it will burst through the clouds again.

Today

Hold your pain, accept it, and watch it change in texture.

December 22

Over time, grief changes. It becomes less sharp, less jagged. It is still with you, but it transmutes, becoming the fuel that inspires you. If you feel this dawning, know that loss has the power to change you, just as love has the power to uplift you. And if you are still very much in the darkness of grief, know that the dawn will come one small ray at a time.

Today

Be patient. Your grief will gradually begin to shift.

December 23

Sometimes, you start to feel a hint of happiness, a small smile, a brief moment of joy—and then you feel guilty: *How can I feel good when my loved one is gone?* You deserve to embrace life, to have glimmers of goodness. Your loved one wants you to accept your birthright of peacefulness. Living well is a testimony to the love that endures.

Today

Even if it is just the briefest glint of light, let happiness shine without guilt.

December 24

Anticipation of a holiday can often be more excruciating than the day itself. Keep your mind focused on this moment and this moment only. Tomorrow is not here yet, and yesterday is gone. All you have is today.

Today

Wiggle your toes to keep you aware of your body in this moment.

December 25

Holidays can be heartbreaking when you are missing an important person. Remember that this holiday is about birth and new beginnings. Just as your loved one transitioned to a new place, you too are transitioning into a new you. You will get through this day, just as you get through each and every day.

Today

Embrace the mystery of birth.

December 26

After you have gotten through a major holiday, you might find that you are exhausted. If you experience a kind of physical and emotional collapse, know that this is normal. Energy moves in cycles, and your energy may be severely depleted.

Today

Give yourself permission to rest and take a nap.

December 27

Grief makes you feel like you're going crazy. Being forgetful, crying at the drop of a hat, losing things, having trouble concentrating, and getting overwhelmed are normal aspects of the process. You will not always feel exactly as you do today . . . Feelings (like life) are impermanent. They will change, expand, heal, and recycle.

Today

Try watching the process from the balcony of your mind—watch the feelings rise and fall and say, "Oh yes, this is what grief does."

December 28

Many people believe that once they've survived a year of grief, they will begin to feel better. For some, this may be true. However, for many, the second year is when the grief really settles into the bones. The pain is undiluted (the fog of grief is gone), which brings a deep sorrow. Do not be surprised if this happens. Ride the wave of it and know that each year will be slightly different than the one before it.

Today

Be open to the second year and beyond, letting grief take you where it needs to.

December 29

There is a Hindu parable that beautifully illustrates transcendence: A guru wanted to teach his student about how to manage pain. He asked the student to first put a handful of salt into a cup and drink it (bitter!). Then he asked the student to put a handful of salt into the nearby lake and drink from it (fresh!). The guru told his student, "The pain of life is pure salt. The amount of pain remains the same, but the bitterness we taste depends on the size of the container we put the pain in. So when you are in pain, the best thing you can do is enlarge your perspective. Become a lake."

Today

Reflect on how you can become a bigger container for your pain. Reflect on how you can become a lake.

December 30

When memories of your loved one begin to fill you with happiness and gratitude rather than searing pain, then you know that you're starting to transcend. If that hasn't happened yet for you, be patient. If it has happened, then savor your blessed memories.

Today

Know that it's possible to feel pain and joy simultaneously.

December 31

Alfred, Lord Tennyson once wrote, "'Tis better to have loved and lost, / Than never to have loved at all——" Remember that loss is the price tag for loving . . . and ultimately, it's worth the price. Imagine life without having known and loved your dear one. The miracle is that you loved, that love is with you eternally. Turn grief back into the love from whence it came.

Today

Hold this blessing close to your heart—love is with you and part of you now and forever.

Special Trigger Days

Any day can be a tough day when it comes to grief. The most ordinary Wednesday can be a day that knocks the breath out of you. However, there are undeniable trigger days, which are almost certain to be particularly poignant. The anticipation of these days can turn out to be harder than the day itself. Likewise, the aftereffects of trigger days can be exhausting.

The following reflections are for the days you will encounter during the year that may present an extra challenge for you.

On Your Birthday

This is a day in which you might have celebrated together. Perhaps you feel "less than" because your special someone isn't here to honor you and celebrate with you. Hold in your heart that your loved one wishes you a happy day. Know that you're still here to accumulate birthdays for a reason.

Today

Light a candle today as a way of symbolically including your loved one in your day. Be open to discovering some of the reasons why you're still alive.

On Your Loved One's Birthday

It can be especially painful to acknowledge that your loved one isn't here to experience any more birthdays. Hold your sorrow, and pair that with the miracle that they were ever born at all. Imagine how your life would have been diminished if they hadn't been here, for however long or short a period of time.

Today

Consider buying a gift in honor of your loved one, an item that you can donate. Let your generosity reflect the gift that you received in the birth of your loved one.

On Your Loved One's Death Day (Angelversary)

The anniversary of transitioning, of leaving the body, of death—the angelversary—can be overwhelming. It's not uncommon to feel blue for weeks or even months before the date, sometimes without realizing why. You don't want to celebrate a day of death, and yet it's a day that needs to be acknowledged. Remember that your loved one's life is more than their death. Whether their passing was traumatic or prolonged, whether it was public or private, it still pales in comparison to a life that touched your own. Anniversaries are about honoring a beautiful life, acknowledging the loss, and confirming that your relationship has transformed to one of spirit and inner knowing.

Let all of your feelings arise, and see this day as another occasion to honor their impact on your life.

Today

Write a letter to your dear one on their departure day. Keep a collection of these annual letters. Honor this powerful and poignant day by nurturing your connection in some way.

Mother's Day

Whether you are a mother who lost a child or a child who lost a mother, this day can be bittersweet. This day can also be complicated if you didn't receive the mothering that you deserved or if you are estranged from your adult child. Hold the complexities in your heart and think of all the nourishing, nurturing energies in your life that surround and hold you.

Today

Feel nurturing love shine upon you and out from within you.

Father's Day

Whether you are a father who lost a child or a child who lost a father, this day can cause your heart to ache. You might have even longed for a relationship with your father (or adult child) that didn't come to pass. Hold the complicated realities of love in your heart, and know that you are being supported in both seen and unseen ways.

Today

Imagine that your heart is full with love and generosity.

FOR WIDOWS AND WIDOWERS

On Your Wedding Anniversary

This is supposed to be a day of celebration, of happiness. And yet, now it is a reminder of your deep and profound loss. While it's important to acknowledge your sorrow, also allow yourself to honor the joy of having been married to your dear one. The years that you shared together, with all of the highs and lows, are imprinted within you.

Today

Remember the beautiful, ordinary days of living with and loving your spouse. Take the time to look through photographs of happy times together.

On the Day Your Child Weds but Your Spouse Isn't with You

This is a day of joy for your child. And yet, it's also a day of keen awareness of someone's absence. Hold open the possibility that your spouse is with you all in spirit and memory. Let love be the theme of the day.

Today

Hold both love and loss in your heart, letting love claim your attention. Make sure that your spouse is mentioned and remembered on this special occasion.

FOR BEREAVED PARENTS

On the Day Your Child Would Have Graduated

You probably anticipated this day with a mixture of emotions. And even now, you may feel sorrow that your child isn't graduating. You might even feel some envy that other children are continuing to live their normal lives, that other parents don't know your pain. Although you cannot know why your child died, you can know that you will be connected through all eternity. They have graduated to another realm, and you too will follow in their footsteps one day.

Today

Every person is on a journey. Wish them all well.

FOR ADULT ORPHANS

On the Day You Wed but Your Parent Isn't There to See It

This is a day of joy and celebration for you, and yet you are painfully aware of the absence of one or both of your parents. Sorrow creeps into your heart even as you prepare for a momentous occasion in your life. Know that all of your loved ones surround you in a circle of spiritual support.

Today

Light a candle on the wedding altar to symbolize anyone dear to you who isn't physically present at your ceremony.

On the Day You Have a Child but Your Parent Isn't There to Become a Grandparent

You have just welcomed a new, precious person into your life. The love in your heart feels full to bursting. And yet, your baby will not get to know their grandparent. You may find that you feel a special connection to your parent as you become a link between the generations. Feel your parent watching over you, offering their blessing.

Today

Whisper to your baby a story about the legacy of their grandparents.

Hope for the Future

It may be difficult to imagine a future, but every day you are growing into it. Be open to mystery, to compassion, and to deep love keeping you tethered to something more.

I wish you peace on the journey . . .

May you let grief wash over you in waves, ebbing and flowing.

May you embrace every feeling with tenderness and compassion.

May you reach out to other people who know the pain of a broken heart.

May you savor the fragile joys of life.

May you experience gratitude for the love forever woven into your soul.

Suggested Reading

Alexander, Ronald A. *Wise Mind, Open Mind: Finding Purpose and Meaning in Times of Crisis, Loss, and Change.* Oakland, CA: New Harbinger, 2008.

Bonanno, George A. *The Other Side of Sadness: What the New Science of Bereavement Tells Us About Life After Loss.* New York: Basic Books, 2010.

Brach, Tara. *Radical Acceptance: Embracing Your Life with the Heart of a Buddha.* New York: Bantam Books, 2004.

Bush, Ashley Davis. *Shortcuts to Inner Peace: 70 Simple Paths to Everyday Serenity*. New York: Berkley Books, 2011.

―――. *Transcending Loss: Understanding the Lifelong Impact of Grief and How to Make It Meaningful*. New York: Berkley Books, 1997.

Chödrön, Pema. *When Things Fall Apart: Heart Advice for Difficult Times*. Boston: Shambhala, 2000.

Germer, Christopher K. *The Mindful Path to Self-Compassion: Freeing Yourself from Destructive Thoughts and Emotions*. New York: Guilford Press, 2009.

Grollman, Earl A. *Living When a Loved One Has Died*. Revised edition. Boston: Beacon Press, 1995.

Halifax, Joan. *Being with Dying: Cultivating Compassion and Fearlessness in the Presence of Death*. Boston: Shambhala, 2009.

Hickman, Martha Whitmore. *Healing After Loss: Daily Meditations for Working Through Grief*. New York: Avon Books, 1994.

Hodges, Samuel J. IV, and Kathy Leonard. *Grieving with Hope: Finding Comfort as You Journey Through Loss.* Grand Rapids, MI: Baker Books, 2011.

James, John W., and Russell Friedman. *The Grief Recovery Handbook,: The Action Program for Moving Beyond Death, Divorce, and Other Losses Including Health, Career, and Faith.* 20th anniversary expanded edition. New York: William Morrow, 2009.

Katie, Byron. *Loving What Is: Four Questions That Can Change Your Life.* New York: Three Rivers Press, 2003.

Kumar, Sameet M. *Grieving Mindfully: A Compassionate and Spiritual Guide to Coping with Loss.* Oakland, CA: New Harbinger, 2005.

Kushner, Harold S. *When Bad Things Happen to Good People.* Norwell, MA: Anchor, 2004.

Lesser, Elizabeth. *Broken Open: How Difficult Times Can Help Us Grow.* New York: Villard, 2005.

Mitsch, Raymond R., and Lynn Brookside. 1993. *Grieving the Loss of Someone You Love: Daily Meditations to Help You Through the Grieving Process*. Grand Rapids, MI: Revell, 2014.

Rando, Therese A. *How to Go On Living When Someone You Love Dies*. New York: Bantam, 1991.

Rasmussen, Christina. *Second Firsts: Live, Laugh, and Love Again*. Carlsbad, CA: Hay House, 2013.

Rosof, Barbara D. *The Worst Loss: How Families Heal from the Death of a Child*. New York: Holt, 2005.

Schwiebert, Pat, and Chuck DeKlyen. *Tear Soup: A Recipe for Healing After Loss*. Portland, OR: Grief Watch, 2005.

Staudacher, Carol. *A Time to Grieve: Meditations for Healing After the Death of a Loved One*. San Francisco: Harper 1994.

Tolle, Eckhart. *The Power of Now: A Guide to Spiritual Enlightenment*. Novato, CA: New World Library, 1999.

Wolfelt, Alan D. *Healing a Spouse's Grieving Heart: 100 Practical Ideas After Your Husband or Wife Dies*. Fort Collins, CO: Companion Press, 2003.

———. *Understanding Your Grief: Ten Essential Touchstones for Finding Hope and Healing Your Heart*. Fort Collins, CO: Companion Press, 2004.

Acknowledgments

I am delighted to gratefully acknowledge my superb editor, Caroline Pincus, and my excellent copyeditor, Susie Pitzen, as well as the entire professional team at Red Wheel/Weiser and Conari Press. I deeply appreciate their enthusiasm for this book and all the many ways they helped bring it to fruition.

My literary agent, John Willig, came through for me once again. His ongoing patience and inspired support is like a breath of fresh air.

And a big thank-you to Richard Evans for his invaluable photographic contributions. He rose to the occasion of providing material even when he was struggling with some serious health concerns. It has been a wonderful collaboration.

I am grateful to my husband, Daniel Bush, who encouraged me to begin writing the daily posts for Facebook in 2009. He recognized a need and nudged me to create an environment for daily communication with grievers. It led to a marvelous and fulfilling experience. Daniel is truly my partner in all ways, making it possible for me to do my work in the world.

I also want to thank all the people who have read, commented on, and encouraged the Transcending Loss community on Facebook. It has been an honor to take part in what I consider a very special ministry.

Over the past twenty-five years, I have had the amazing privilege of sitting with hundreds of clients who have known tremendous grief. I thank each of these brave souls for allowing me to accompany them on such a sacred journey. I have learned from them about eternal love and the resilient spirit. They have taught me to blow the dust off of my own life, helping me to see with more clarity and perspective.

In order to remain available to continue with this work, I intentionally keep myself anchored in Divine presence. One way I do that is by being connected to the Society of Saint John the Evangelist. The SSJE monastic brotherhood offers a network of resources and personal connections that keeps me grounded and receptive. Blessed thanks.

To my dear beloved ones who have crossed the thin veil between this world and the next, I love you now and always: Ruth, Pat, Catherine, Calvin C., Willie, Ida, Calvin W., Ingeborg, Joseph, Jonathan, Charlotte, Bella, Sugar, and Hickory.

To my mother, Peyton Lewis, and my father, William Davis, I offer heartfelt gratitude for their consistent love and support throughout my life.

And lastly, I thank the Muse, the Spirit, my North Star, which guides me and inspires me to reach out to those in emotional pain.

About the Author

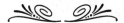

Ashley Davis Bush, LCSW, is the internationally bestselling author of six self-help books, including the classic *Transcending Loss: Understanding the Lifelong Impact of Grief and How to Make It Meaningful.* She has appeared on *The Diane Rehm Show*, MSNBC, Fox News, the Oprah Winfrey Network, and countless radio programs. She has worked as a psychotherapist and grief counselor in both community mental health and private practice for the past 25 years. Visit Ashley online at *www.ashleydavisbush.com*

About the Photographer

Richard Evans, a retired educator, took his first professional job as a photographer in the mid-1970s, creating an exhibit for the New Hampshire Council for the Humanities. His work has been shown in numerous exhibitions and has been published in regional magazines. He has been the recipient of several awards for his photography of animals.

Richard captures his images with the eye of someone who has known grief. After the death of his twenty-five year old son in 2003, it was through photography that he found solace by trying to capture the beauty of the natural world.

Richard lives with his wife Carol in Collier County, Florida.

Mango Publishing, established in 2014, publishes an eclectic list of books by diverse authors—both new and established voices—on topics ranging from business, personal growth, women's empowerment, LGBTQ studies, health, and spirituality to history, popular culture, time management, decluttering, lifestyle, mental wellness, aging, and sustainable living. We were recently named 2019 *and* 2020's #1 fastest growing independent publisher by *Publishers Weekly*. Our success is driven by our main goal, which is to publish high quality books that will entertain readers as well as make a positive difference in their lives.

Our readers are our most important resource; we value your input, suggestions, and ideas. We'd love to hear from you—after all, we are publishing books for you!

Please stay in touch with us and follow us at:

Facebook: Mango Publishing
Twitter: @MangoPublishing
Instagram: @MangoPublishing
LinkedIn: Mango Publishing
Pinterest: Mango Publishing
Newsletter: mangopublishinggroup.com/newsletter

Join us on Mango's journey to reinvent publishing, one book at a time.

9 781573 246675